Fearless Actin

Moving from weakness to strength across the stage

By William R. Cole

Printed in the United States of America

First Printing, 2017
Typeset in Times New Roman 12 pt.

Contents

Introduction

If a performer wants to grow into a confident force, with a relaxed and positive countenance then they need to inhabit a place of inner peace, void of fear.

This book will seek to provide new tools and a common sense approach that will enable an actor to work outside their personal comfort zone and risk in a safe environment that can be created anytime anywhere.

Through behavioral development and strengthening innate performance abilities anyone can easily find a pathway to fulfilled success littered with self-assuredness.

Rather than running from a personal Gettysburg, you will come to view the stage not as a battle waiting to happen but a work-space where you can express your true artist.

Chapter One - No body brings a tomato or a cabbage to theater

You feel your muscles begin to tense, your armpits start to sweat and heart pounds, mouth goes dry and you start to shake, your throat constricts, and you are sure your voice will rise or drop in pitch. A fight or flight response is taking you over, with the emphasis on *FLIGHT*. But what a Neanderthal needed when confronted with a toothy tiger is not what an actor needs in order to play Blanche in "Streetcar". Without release, the impending cataclysm turns into a full scale a panic attack. "Why is my leg trembling?"

But it's too late. Your cue line approaches and the stage manager's hand is felt firmly on the middle of your back getting ready to push . . . you . . . onto the stage . . . under the bright lights . . . in front of . . .THE AUDIENCE.

The moment approaches and you think, "All I need is to say my first line and I'll be okay . . . which is . . . which is . . . WHICH IS??? OMG I CAN'T REMEMBER MY FIRST LINE."

Sound like a nightmare? For many performers 'nightmare' is a benevolent way of putting it. And the sad thing is that 'stage fright' is something that they inflict on themselves. It doesn't have to be this way. There is a way to let go, settle nerves, breathe, center, move with purpose across the boards and speak with authority. For some it will be easy. Others, perhaps, will take work. But it can be conquered. And, perhaps, surprisingly turned around on itself, to work for performers rather than against them.

The first step

Above, I put the words stage + fright together. That is the only time in this book that you will encounter those two words combined one after the other. Together they do not correctly identify what you are dealing with and 99% of the problem is how that elevated excitement encountered prior to stepping out is continually defined as a "bad" thing. The fluttering that comes over you shouldn't be associated with something "scary." Leave that milieu to Steven King or Freddy Kruger. I prefer to refer to these so-called "butterflies" as Stage Audacity.

Look up the word "audacity" in the dictionary and you will find something along the lines of "the willingness to take bold risks." And perhaps even, "impudence." Personally, I like the word impudence as it contains a hint of arrogance about it without being mean-spirited. But more importantly are those words "willingness" and "risk." Without risk there is no "conquer." And yes, risk does have a possibility of threat or danger or failure involved. But a willingness to risk takes both courage and conviction. And if you don't take that first step out onto the stage embracing both, then you are doomed to rinse and repeat.

So how does one go about risking . . . safely? Are you familiar with that trust exercise that is so popular in those corporate team-building seminars? Falling backwards trusting that your mates will catch you before your head crashes into the floor? Budding CEOs are able to let go as they are certain that those behind them will prevent their noggins from flattening on the linoleum. Look down at your own two hands. Place them about a foot from one another facing one another. Now imagine a network of webbing connecting the two of them. There . . .there is a high wire safety net. Yup, you can be that big poofy bag that stunt performers fall into in and all by yourself. Okay, okay - their poofy bag is bigger than that - but we will get into how large you can make it in the pages ahead. But, one step at a time. The first person you have to trust . . . in order to have a willingness to risk and fall . . . is YOU.

Creating Safe Spaces

Haven, refuge, harbor, retreat, shelter, asylum, security, preservation, invulnerability, tranquility, immunity - all these are the antithesis of "risk."

Think of those times when you have felt peaceful and centered. It could be when you are reading, sipping a cup of coffee or lying in a hammock on a summer day under a leafy maple. Close your eyes and lock that place and time into your consciousness. This can become a place you can go to anytime when you sit - quiet, calm, relaxed in both body and mind. Open yourself up to deep breathing, relaxation exercises, yoga, and meditation, anything that works for you that allows you to allow every worry, unease or difficulty slip away. Practice and allow yourself to come to this place . . . this safe space anytime, anywhere. A relaxed state that is readily available is the first tool that any performer should have in their box. If you have one, GREAT, if not, then start building that place to hang your hammock NOW.

If you have a pebble between sock and sole, you stop, unleash and dump it. You cannot take that all important step with confidence if you are limping around with a stone in your shoe. Remove the stone in your shoe. An actor or performer must be able to set aside any distraction. When directing the most powerful note I can give is "leave your personal agenda at the door." This applies to not only the rehearsal process and then the run . . . but also to the actor as an individual. You cannot bring the focus necessary for you to achieve anything if you are carting around today's baggage. A lot of lip service is given to "live in the moment" . . . and it is at the heart of any truly great performance. But if you are consumed with the mundane everyday anxieties of life, then you are unable to give yourself over to that safe space that you need and want to create.

Getting Clear

What is that baggage you are carrying around? Judgments, doubts, insecurities, or seeking the need for approval? A never-ending internal criticism that's stifling your ability to access that calm safe space we call "center." The result is an actor who appears to be filled with static. Messages like "This is a lousy choice" - or - "Does anyone like me?" - or - "I hate this play" will get in the way of whatever you are attempting create, pulling you out of 'the moment" you are living in. You become scattered, unfocused and blocked. No wonder fear and uncertainty have the room to creep in.

Living with uncertainty and doubt is a part of the human condition. We make judgments about ourselves and those around us, every second of every day. As an experiment . . . try taking a walk down a busy street, through a shopping mall, or wander around a park during a sunny summer day. As you amble about, do so with a focused awareness of each and every time your brain makes a judgment. You will be amazed at how often, and the intensity level, with which you pass verdict on everything around you as it passes by. Part of this exercise is an excellent way for an actor to gain sensitivity and awareness of what it means to be human, and can be used to build character. But the point of this particular stroll is to shed light on those things you unconsciously live with that aren't needed when building a tabula rasa on which to chalk. Judgments you pass on others are usually judgments about yourself. You need to erase counterproductive thoughts, negative judgments and unnecessary distractions when you walk into your safe space. You can always pick the old worn valise on your way OUT the door. But when you are walking into your calm place . . . leave it at the doorway. It won't go anywhere without you so stop worrying about it.

Resistance

We fear change. Yup, that's another one of those pesky 'human condition' things that everyone deals with. But as a performer it slows your process to a crawl and makes risk almost impossible. So even though you've discovered a place of safety . . . and have clarity with a calm state of mind . . . you have to have a willingness to be open to the river. Change has to have the freedom to flow through you. It is the only way that you will discover new vistas and emotional landscapes. Indeed if you are stuck behind a large rock before the looming scary rapids you will never get to that spot where the north fork and the south fork come together. And even then, if you are unwilling to risk the next set of rapids how will you find other tributaries that will deliver you to the ocean? Come on, if you aren't able to let the flow take you, then your destination will be the riverbank.

s to Risk

If you want to play with the big dogs you have to get off the porch. So the first step was to stand up out of that old, weathered rocking chair. Now you're standing at the top of the stairsteps and ready to get into the game. Good for you! The potential that lies in front of you in the back yard is infinite. Commitment ALWAYS involves taking risks. And if you are going to risk . . . go all the way and make the BIG risks. If you are open to change and realize that you are in a safe sound space then there isn't room for "mistakes." In fact there is another word that actors and performers need to strike from their vocabulary. There are NO SUCH THINGS as mistakes. Realize a 'mistake' is simply a judgment and a doubt that you are making that doesn't serve you. So see, if you are incapable of making a "mistake" then no one can judge you adversely. So what are you afraid of? Shining?

What ARE you afraid of?

Do you think that you are scared of failure? Is that what you think stops you at the edge of the curtain and keeps you from taking that big step? Well I hate to tell you but we encounter failure every day. But that's not what we are frightened of. Actually we're afraid of being seen, . . .of being seen in truth. This is the "naked in front of the world" that paralyzes. And then, of course, is that possibility of rejection, of not doing it "right," and of being imperfect. Forbid that we show people who we really are, of being a blunder, exposing that weird birthmark and consequently, having people not like us.

And yet . . . here's a cold naked truth: You *will* be rejected - lots of times, just for being who you are. That's the risk you take being fully invested in life - in love, in your art, in acting, in dancing, in putting butt out there, in painting, in singing, in all forms of creation. You are constantly revealing who you are and giving a part of yourself away in everything you do. And that might mean that some people just won't get you or like you or be interested in you.

So what? You're not doing it for them. You SHOULD BE doing it for yourself. And when you really start to live in truth . . . Here it is . . . Pay heed to this . . . You won't care what other people think because there's no greater gift than giving of yourself, with the risk that in doing so, you might be rejected. Trust me - you will be. Rejected. But that's called life, and it's why we're here.

What then could it be that what we're really scared of ? Could it be success? Of how powerful we can be, how spectacular and delightful and competent and talented we already are? And then, ironically, we are scared of success because that could mean that with success comes the possibility that we may get rejected or not "liked." It means putting our private selves out there in a very public way. Success equals overcoming the tapes that run in our heads that tell us all the reasons we aren't, and can't possibly be, a success. But what if I told you that overcoming that negative judgment is success. Success is facing all destructive urges to prove otherwise stepping into the possibility that it is better to attempt, to risk, to be seen, and to somehow fall short (of what?) than to not be seen at all.

In other words — What would you do if you KNEW you could not fail.

Chapter Two - Dance like no one is watching . . . but witn mirrors

It's one of those songs that just moves you. It hits the radio and you just cannot sit. You have to get up and shake it shake it shake it. Abandonment. And why not? No one is watching. Except for Mom up in heaven who is looking down from above wondering what in the hell has gotten into you. Oh and that guy in the building across the way who can peer right in on you since the curtains aren't drawn. Yeah dance with abandon LIKE no one is watching. Even if they are. Confidence. That's what it's really called. That complete and utter non-judgmental state that you find yourself in when you are joyously possessed.

"I was doing theater. It was all I ever wanted to do. It was so much fun . . . it's the greatest education in the world."
Jeffrey Tambor

Learn to enjoy the process

Performing ain't easy. It is full of all sorts of tough hard work. Work that can take weeks of rehearsal in studio and work at home alone. It can be a struggle to find choices that work for you. Slogging through pages of dialogue and monologue to get your ass off book. Figuring out how your character walks and talks may be fraught with pitfalls. I remember playing Talthybius in a production of Euripides' "Trojan Women." Four weeks of rehearsal figuring out how to be the sympathetic voice yet stoical statesman at the same time. Of how to hold myself like an esteemed political when in truth he knew he was merely a messenger . . . how to realize the internal struggle he had between his anger toward his betters and the duty-bound moral code that ruled his life.

It was hard work. And I was satisfied with the idea that I was doing a pretty good job of it. Until on final dress, the director pulled me to one side and gave me a single note. Which was "It just isn't working. We need to try something else." ACK! I freaked out. All that hard work and analysis, the physicality of the statesman and I get "try something." What!?! Try "what?" The director wasn't offering any help and I felt that I was now a helium balloon with a small slowly leaking puncture that was threatening to rip open a hole that would send me careening around the room. Until . . . later that night as I pouring my anxiety into a glass of whiskey, another actor from a different company took the bar stool beside me and asked how things were going over in Troy. I gave him the sad, somber tale and he told me something that changed my life in the theater forever. He said, "So, then you get to do whatever you want. You have complete freedom to try something else. That's what the director's note meant. Especially since he doesn't have anything specific to offer you. Have FUN with it. Do something different every performance. Just do it honestly."

WOW! Have fun with it? What a concept! From that moment onward I vowed to approach all my work in the theater with joy. After all, the work itself was/is a steep climb and challenging enough to take care of the blood, sweat and tears. Why not enjoy every moment of it. Relish in the chance to do it. Celebrate putting it on the line. Dance with abandonment even during those moments when standing stoically in the background observing the action on stage without being "seen." Know that being alive in the moment is riveting.

Focus - Trust - Confidence

Stage Audacity is achieved by focusing on your true purpose. Being confident that you are contributing something of value. Trusting that what you are involving the spectators in is worthy of their attention.

You've got to have confidence and trust in your cast. You have to have confidence and trust in your director, in your editor. It's such a team effort; I really think you have to pull yourself out of it and just trust. I think the number one thing you can do is just trust everyone around you. Reid Scott

We have already addressed "focus" in the previous chapter but it does demand a bit of clarification here as well. Leaving your baggage at the door is the first step in allowing yourself to bring attention to your center and focus on what it is you are about to do. Focus allows you to let all else fall away and concentrate on stepping from the outside into the present and bring all your senses and heightened awareness to the moment. Sharply focusing yourself allows you to take your thumb and forefinger together to flick that little devil that sits on your shoulder commenting to you on all that you are doing, off into the wings behind you. Sending them back to the dressing room to wait patiently for you until you have finished what you have set out to do.

This also allows you to then have confidence in the work. Again there is no "good" or "bad" work. It just "is." If you've done the work then you are bringing your talent and clarity of vision to bear. Being confident in the knowledge that the work is enough. The human mind is an amazing thing. The term "steel trap" wasn't coined out of thin air.

You are capable of remembering every page and every word that was put before you. The movement and physical interactions you map out become muscle memory. All of the analysis of what makes your character tick is a study never taken in vain. And the big choices you've uncovered will take you on an extraordinary journey from opening curtain to final bow.

Out of this confidence comes trust. Trust that you know the story of the work and are comfortable speaking that story. Trust that you are comfortably present in the moment and that you are attentively listening and reacting (99% of the time the 'script' will flow out of you if you trust that comfort). Trust that your peers on stage have your back. They are your safety net should you discover a hole torn in your own. Trust in your honesty. Trust in theirs.

Focus, trust and confidence are the foundation of acting fearlessly. With these three keys you are enabling yourself and your fellow actors to simply . . . have fun.

Titanic - If you are a Rose, move over, there is room on that door for a Jack too

Disaster WILL strike. It's a given. Your expectation should be that at any time something will go awry. That's why they call it LIVE Theater. Another quick story. My director chose to also take on a role in a production of "The Goodbye Girl." During a run, her entrance line was delivered and . . . she was a no show. We improvised our way around the missed entrance and came back around to the cue. Again . . no actor. Finally the mom, Paula, said, "I wonder what is keeping her?" . . . walked off stage . . . grabbed the director Lisa (playing daughter Quinn) and pulled her onto the set.

The play proceeded. After bows backstage, we asked her what the hell happened and why did Lisa/Quinn leave us hanging. She came back with, "Well you guys dropped some dialogue and I wanted you to go back and pick it up. I wasn't going to come on until you picked it back up and fixed it." Okay, so Lisa didn't have our backs and perhaps that was trust misplaced. But the point is that we - those of us in the moment out in the world of the play - stayed in the moment - treated it honestly – trusted each other - and no one was the wiser. So was this a Titanic moment in need of a life raft? No, not at all. While that night wasn't a clean run of the show, we did deliver a show to our audience that evening that was perhaps more risky and alive than any of the others put before the lights during the entire run. So give up on the idea of perfect performance. Lines will be dropped. Light cues screwed up. Inadvertent sounds may distract (please spare me crying babies). But if you view all impending disasters as challenges rather than mistakes . . . to be faced with all the preparation provided with you by the work done over the course of the process . . . then it is extremely unlikely that Jack will end up frozen on the bottom of the Atlantic. (unless, of course, that is how the story as written by the playwright is meant to end).

An Actor Prepares - Why we rehearse

If you do the work - then you are prepared to take on the world. And Bill Shakespeare said it best . . . "all the world IS a stage." If you are prepared then even the worst of disasters can be met fearlessly with calm, centered Stage Audacity. As an actor I always endeavored to get 'off book' as quickly as I could. And to nail down both lines and cues to the point where I could toss the script aside. Granted I still needed to make notations in it regarding blocking and direction . . . but in terms of getting the playwright out of my head I needed to get he/she into it as quickly as I could. I will reiterate something I referred to earlier. Become as comfortable as you can with speaking the story not the script. Listen and react. 99% of the time the playwright's words will flow out of you. BUT (and this is a big one) in order to become confident in the performance expect that you are not going to be word perfect. It is okay to be live and in the moment. Just be honest in that moment. And the way to achieve this confidence is to learn the script backwards, forwards and sideways. Then, somewhat ironically, forget it. If the actors are onstage listening and reacting to each other . . . the script will out.

Different directors have different approaches to blocking. As a young actor blocking always was a way for me to memorize script. As a director it allowed me to set tableaus that illuminated the story. There are those who will disagree but I also feel, as both actor and director, that blocking shouldn't be so constrictive to a performance that any actor on stage is no longer fluid. Rather, the blocking should serve as yet another safety net that allows risk in a safe environment. Sometimes an unexpected change in blocking during a performance can raise the stakes if the performance is suffering from a loss of energy. Everyone must be adaptable and non-resistant to change in order to accommodate. I also feel that performance can (and perhaps should) be simply an extension of rehearsal. A safe place where new approaches can be investigated. Remember all along the way, that there are no "mistakes" in the theater.

As a young actor I also invested a large part of myself and my character in costume. For me the ceremony of pulling my wardrobe off the hangers and slipping into pants, shirt, coat and shoes was like a shedding myself and encasing myself into my character. All well and good. It served its purpose back then. But I came to realize that was simply a crutch and I was basically creating artificiality in my work. I came to understand that I was hiding behind the makeup and the costume and that was a roadblock to truly and honestly embodying the work. So I started to do something else that I think is something every actor who wants to utilize fearless acting in their process needs to do. I started a journal written in the voice of the character. A life story or biography as it were. This allowed me to have an intimate knowledge of why the character did what they did. What brought them to this place and this time. Over time it evolved into a way of approaching the building of a fully realized character that I could trust. A character that I no longer had to pull on like a second skin but rather one who inhabited me. One that pulled ME on like a rumbled suit coat. It was not only a more honest approach to the work but also gave me a stronger confidence allowing my private self to be naked in front of the audience without fear. In other words, this confidence provided me with the self-assuredness needed to permit myself to simply trust my work.

Hopefully you see that diligence, time and joyful work will provide you with the certitude that you have something worthwhile that demands to be seen by an audience. And stepping out of the wings onto the stage is nothing to be reticent about. Rather you should be like a race horse anticipating the opening of the gate.

Trust no one but your selves

"You are NOT the words of your critics. Take any valid feedback as an opportunity for growth and flush the rest of it out of your being. Our work is too important to allow anyone to sidetrack us. You are too important to be diminished."
Jackie Moore

One of the truly wonderful things about the art of theater is that it is a collaborative form. A monologue is just a hollow voice in the dark if not for the person who designed the lighting plot and the person sitting in the booth pushing the sliders. The rehearsal process helps the actor find all the warts and hairy lumps that need to be exposed in order for the audience to have an emotional response. But it is also necessary to build, block-by-block, a camaraderie amongst all the integral parts into the making of a whole. In the opening sentences I referred to a stage manager with their hand placed firmly on the middle of your back. I lied. SM's are not there to push you onto the stage (though a good SM will literally throw your ass out there if you are hiding in wings waiting for the cast to go back and pickup a few dropped lines). Rather, that hand is a reassuring pat on the back to let you know that everyone is in this together. Even the solo performer has a supporting cast behind them without whom there would be no performance. I liken everyone in the backstage to Willie in "Happy Days." Mostly silent but steadfastly there beside Winnie as she goes on about her day. Therein lies an actor's truest safest space. Their peers and comrades all looking to have each others' back. Encouraging one another to push the other, creating something new and alive in each moment shared together.

There is one other collaborator who must not be ignored or forgotten. The audience. It may surprise you to know that they are your best and biggest support group. They WANT you to be excellent. They WANT to see the result of all you have poured into the heart of your performance. They have no interest in judging you and more often than not cannot wait to repay your courage with applause. Most of them cannot for the life of them imagine doing what you do. And here's a surprising truth . . . 90% of them hold you in awe. If they only knew how simple it was to have the audacity to walk out on stage and stand before them. But we can keep that our secret. A part of our fraternity and sorority if you will. That is what hides behind those two Greek masks. It only takes a dash of arrogance and a measure of trust to walk out to the center downstage and speak. So trust them. They are interested in throwing neither tomatoes nor old cabbages. They are in your corner. They are there for YOU.

Chapter Three - Speak the speech I pray thee, trippingly off the tongue

So you're an actor . . . now ACT . . . NEXT!

Thank you . . . don't call us . . . we'll call you.

Everyone gets nervous at auditions. An audition is so far removed from being in a production with 7 other actors . . . and a director . . . designer(s) . . . stage manager . . . dresser . . . Wait a minute . . . Is it? *No.* Not really. Well. *Yes,* the auditor is automatically in a position of judge. And you only have two minutes to turn it on . . . then off. Not to mention your headshot is old and resume is about a year out of date. There are so many mistakes that can happen during that two minutes. Huh? THERE ARE NO MISTAKES IN THEATER!

Preparation

The biggest problem an actor must deal with in the audition process is overcoming their fears of judgment and rejection by the auditor . . . no no no NO . . . the biggest problem an actor faces in the audition process is facing fears of SELF-judgment and twisting themselves into a bizarre knot in order to give them swift kicks afterwards for not taking the time and energy to put their best self forward. So stop that.

Why and how can you stop pitting yourself against yourself? Here's a wild suggestion. Take your tried and true audition pieces and toss 'em. Been there - done that. Even YOU are bored. Start fresh. Begin anew. Get a piece of paper and make a list of all your passions. Rather than leafing through a book of monologues to find what you

· amazing piece that will guarantee landing the …art making a list of all of the themes that inspire your passions, however major or minuscule. Then seek out audition pieces that allow you to express that passion. The more zany or out there the better, that's a smashing way to give a refreshing and unique performance in the audition room. But it will be coming from YOU. The real YOU. It will reflect YOUR zeal and spirit. Your honest expression of self, shown through the lens of a character who shares what excites you. That is why and how to excite the auditor and make your two minutes stay with them for days (maybe even years) after.

A great example of this passionate topical piece that might speak to personally to you could be Edmund in Lear (Act 1 Sc 2).

"I only worship what's natural, not what's manmade. Why should I let myself be tortured by manmade social customs that deprive me of my rights simply because I was born twelve or fourteen months later than my older brother? Why do they call me "bastard" and "lowlife" when I'm just as gifted in mind and body as legitimate children? Why do they call us bastards" and "lowlifes?" At least we bastards were conceived in a moment of passionate lust rather than in a dull, tired marriage bed, where half-sleeping parents monotonously churn out a bunch of sissy kids. All right then, legitimate brother Edgar, I have to have your lands. Our father loves me just as much as the legitimate Edgar. What a nice word that is, "legitimate"! Well, my legitimate Edgar, if this letter works and my plan succeeds, Edmund the lowlife will beat the legitimate. Look out, I'm on my way up. Three cheers for bastards!"

Don't be afraid to edit it for time. It matters not if you are male or female. (In fact a women delivering the above honestly and passionately would be an audition that the auditor(s) would be one remembered at the end of the day). Often audition pieces are chosen simply because they are "expected." Gods forbid that an 18 year old girl do anything other than Rebecca Gibbs from "Our Town," If she were to walk in and nail 2 minutes of Ricky Roma from "Glengarry Glen Ross" that would be the audition I would remember for the referred to above years to come. Most auditors should care more about the ability to deliver the emotional content than the context.

That said, please take this with a certain measure of salt and give it very careful consideration as it can be taking on huge risk in a somewhat unsafe space. Namely, such a choice can rub some auditors the wrong way. So, if you choose this route, only do so if you are completely confident in what you are presenting in that two minutes. An 18 year old boy trying to pitch an 80 year old King named Lear may be simply too distracting for the auditor to wrap their head around and you end up fighting a vertical rock face climb without enough time to place your pitons and hook on any carabineers.

So, may I suggest, when looking for an unexpected, untraditional monologue, you may want to consider sources other than plays. Authors of popular fiction offer first person voices in a large variety of characters. Here's a great excerpt from Neil Gaiman's "American Gods"

"I can believe things that are true and things that aren't true and I can believe things where nobody knows if they're true or not. I can believe in Santa Claus and the Easter Bunny and the Beatles and Marilyn Monroe and Elvis and Mister Ed. Listen – I believe that people are perfectible,

that knowledge is infinite, that the world is run by secret banking cartels and is visited by aliens on a regular basis, nice ones that look like wrinkled lemurs and bad ones who mutilate cattle and want our water and our women.

I believe that the future sucks and I believe that the future rocks and I believe that one day White Buffalo Woman is going to come back and kick everyone's ass. I believe that all men are just overgrown boys with deep problems communicating and that the decline in good sex in America is coincident with the decline in drive-in movie theaters from state to state. I believe that all politicians are unprincipled crooks and I still believe that they are better than the alternative. I believe California is going to sink into the sea when the big one comes, while Florida is going to dissolve into madness and alligators and toxic waste. I believe that antibacterial soap is destroying our resistance to disease so that one day we'll all be wiped out by the common cold like Martians in War of the Worlds.

I believe in absolute honesty and sensible lies. I believe in a woman's right to choose, a baby's right to live, that while all human life is sacred here's nothing wrong with the death penalty if you can trust the legal system implicitly, and that no one but a moron would ever trust the legal system. I believe that life is a game, that life is a cruel joke, and that life is what happens when you're alive and that you might as well lie back and enjoy it."

I edited that and it is still way too long. But hopefully it stands as an example of a monologue that contains a wide range of big risky choices taken from an unexpected source. And it should also shed some light on the idea that to find the perfect audition piece you must be willing to dig a little.

The point is, no matter where your scripted words come from, look for material with which you are emotionally intimate. You have a personal backstory that can be tapped into and that will allow you to go a long way to fully fleshing out a character in your audition. Personally, I know what it's like to be the runt of a litter. So, if I can find material that speaks about being treated like a second class citizen in the family, then more than likely I can have a personal connection with the piece, speaking with an authority that will make a powerful impact. So for me . . . here's Tyrion Lannister from "Game of Thrones":

Do you remember cousin Orson? Orson Lannister? He used to sit all day in the garden, crushing beetles with a rock. [imitating Orson] Kun, kun, kun! (a beat) Nothing made me happier than sitting with Orson.. Laughing at another person's misery was the only thing that made me feel like everyone else. (another beat) I was curious. Why was he smashing all those beetles? What did he get out of it? "Orson, why are you smashing all those beetles?" He gave me an answer. "Smash the beetles! Kun kun kun!" I wasn't deterred. Certainly I had the wherewithal to unravel the mysteries that lay at the heart of a moron. So I went to Maester Valeric's library. Turns out far too much has been written about great men and not nearly enough about morons. Doesn't seem right. In any case, I found nothing that illuminated the nature of Orson's affliction or the reason behind his relentless beetles slaughter. So I went back to the source. I may not have been able to speak with Orson, but I could observe him, watch him, the way men watch animals to come to a deeper understanding of their behavior. [Tyrion picks up a bug off the floor] And as I watched, I became more and more sure of it: there was something happening there. His face was like the page of a book written in a language I didn't understand, but he wasn't mindless, he had his reasons. And I became possessed with knowing what they were. I began spending inordinate amounts of time watching him. I would eat my lunch in the garden, chewing my mutton to the music of "kun kun kun." And when I wasn't watching him, I was thinking about him. Father droned on about the family legacy . . . and I thought about Orson's beetles. I read the histories of Targaryen conquests. Did I hear dragon wings? No, I heard "kun kun kun." And I still couldn't figure out why he was doing it. And I had to know because it was horrible, that all these beetles would be dying for no reason.

It filled me with dread. Piles and piles of them, years and years of them. How many countless living, crawling things smashed, dried out, and returned to the dirt? In my dreams, I found myself standing on a beach made of beetle husks stretching as far as the eye can see. I woke up, crying, weeping for their shattered little bodies. I tried to stop Orson once. He just pushed me aside with a "kun", and just kept on smashing.

Unfortunately, this example is way too long for a standard audition monologue but (and again) it is a great example of an examined life, with a personal connection. This requires knowing and accepting yourself without reservation and negative judgments. Do I need to say "Confidence - Trust – Focus?" I didn't think so.

An audition is not a performance. Rather it is a director or producer's vehicle and they are looking for a driver. Did you use your turn signal when making a left? Come to a full stop or just a rolling one? Can you make the tires squeal without putting the car into tailspin? And what if we spook a deer into jumping out in front of you!? Is Bambi's mom in safe hands?

"But Liam, you said that no one was 'judging me'. What's up with that?" Just trust that a good director WANTS you to do a great job. We are in your corner. We want to see your best and see if we can help bring your best out of you. A director/auditor may ask you to take a different approach to your piece. This doesn't mean that your work was lacking. It simply is a way the person in the director chair sticks a toe in the water testing to see how easily you take direction . . . or are adaptable to change. Cold? Hot? Lukewarm? Take a risk!

Callbacks are usually cold readings. You may be asked to take on several different roles and work with several different actors. You may be familiar with the script or not. No matter. The most important thing in doing a cold reading is listening to the other actors and responding honestly to what you are hearing. Perhaps even more importantly, taking direction from the auditor without fear of making a mistake. Don't worry about tripping up over a line or word error. During this type of audition the auditor is more interested in seeing what chemistry develops than a word-perfect delivery. Look at your scene partner when speaking. And when you are listening to them. Obviously pacing will not be at performance level. But do your best to simply glance at the page to get your words so that you can spark some energy and flow that is not dependent upon the script.

Risk

Make big choices. Not only in a prepared audition but especially in cold readings. Again, this is not performance and obviously the script analysis that is undertaken during the rehearsal process doesn't even enter into the picture. Rather what a great opportunity to be spontaneous without concern or worry as to whether or not the choices you are making . . . in the spur of the moment . . . are "correct."

Where can mistakes made? Gosh, where have we heard this before? No mistakes in theater. An audition is perhaps more "live" and more immediate than any performance. Big choices are a great way to generate chemistry and motion in what can otherwise be a static situation. If the auditor feels that you might be going off the rails by making that "big choice, trust that they will stop you and give you the opportunity to show them how well you take direction . . . how adaptable you are to change . . . and how fearless you are when it comes to re-attacking the reading. ATTACK ! What a great word to keep in the back of your mind when you find yourself with script in hand and no real idea of what is coming or what to do next.

Rejection

You walk out of auditions and/or callbacks and feel like you absolutely NAILED IT. And guess what - you DID! If you did everything you set out to and exceeded your own expectations then what more can anyone ask of you? They simply have to cast you cause you're perfect for the role. Well here's another little secret that I will pass along. Please don't tell any directors you may know that I broke this solemn vow we all have promised to never tell. Usually after auditions I have two . . .or maybe even three possible casts. And more than likely you are in one of them – but not all. So, if I opt to go with cast "B" . . . and you are in cast "A" then you won't get the call you were hoping for. Understand the rejection isn't about you. It's about a somewhat arbitrary decision that has more to do with the bigger picture individual faces that comprise the snapshot. There are bazillion reasons why a director might not extend an offer to you. Recently a company in Seattle did a production of "Julius Caesar" with an all female cast. So Mr. Man, do you think your audition was such a huge failure that they couldn't imagine you as Cassius? Or could it have more to do with something you have absolutely no control over . . . the fact that you have a Mr. in front of your name and not a Ms.? When you get that "Thanks, you were great but we've decided ___ phone call" please do not take it as a review or condemnation of your work. Let me repeat/rephrase a snippet that you read in Chapter One. You're not auditioning for them. You are auditioning for yourself. Truth is that there's no greater gift than giving of yourself . . . with the risk that in doing so, you might be rejected. Walk into any audition with Audacity and walk out with Impudence. You will be a winner, regardless of the ultimate outcome. Putting 110% into the audition should be your reward, a role offering will be the icing on your chocolate cake. AND . . . here's the kicker . . . you do not have to take every role that is offered you. If you can't imagine yourself working with "that" director . . . or committing to the rehearsal/performance schedule . . . or investing yourself in the character that is being offered . . . do yourself and the production a favor and let the person making the offer know that while you truly appreciate the opportunity . . . for personal reasons you find that you must pass.

- …re your audition in exactly the same way you would prepare for a full run of a show. Put together a backstory for your character with as much information about who, what, where, when or why as you would for any production. Where was your character three minutes ago? How much cash money do they have in their pocket at that moment? What did they have for breakfast that morning? Do they have a date later that evening? Then, when you walk in, focus specifically on the exact moment you are in. Be honest and you will spontaneous create a delivery that isn't controlled and flows as naturally as you want it to.

- Never ever ever say "I'm sorry." You are only drawing attention to something only YOU see as wrong. THERE ARE NO MISTAKES IN THEATER. If you must, simply pause and start again, with the same conviction that you walked in with. If you have made that commitment, to yourself then you will always be right. I even suggest you refrain from asking if you can "start again." Just pause. Back yourself up. And do it. Then if the auditor stops you and asks you to either start again - or let's you know that they have seen enough - don't take it personally. There is no element of shame involved.

- When you do take your leave - do so graciously. Regardless of how you may be judging how the audition went. Your professional demeanor will be remembered. If not now, then the next time you might find yourself in front of the same auditor.

- There is no judgment that you need to be c
Leave your personal baggage and that "Min
who sits on your shoulder at the door. If you
given then the aforementioned polite exit sho

- Look polished but wear clothing that allows you to inhabit and embrace your audition. Be comfortable, this ain't the runway. You may want to suggest character via your choice of clothing. But don't costume yourself. Think "The Voice" auditions and not "American Idol." Looking outrageous is not going to make you memorable . . . if it does, then that big silly hat you decided to wear will not be memorable in a good way.

- RISK and be flexible. Be open to change or press on confidently with your work regardless of where you THINK the audition is going. Bold choices are far more impressive than safe expectable ones. Referring to the above - a big floppy hat is NOT a "bold" choice. Starting an audition facing upstage and then turning down . . . or inhabiting a character fully who goes through a change in the moment . . . or actually "seeing" that knife hanging in the air before you and questioning its existence . . . is.

Chapter Four - Alchemy or how to make your own light saber

Luke Skywalker, piloting an X-wing fighter borrowed from the Rebellion, destroys the Death Star, and now is hailed as a hero. But Luke only sought to get behind the controls and support the Freedom Fighters, tapping into skills honed during runs he made against the occasional Womp-Rat on Tatooine. Now Luke is getting a big ass medallion hung around his neck and he is feeling the stirrings in this supposed mystical energy known as the "Force" that some old hermit back home told him about. This farm boy turned fighter pilot is now beginning to suspect that his destiny lies along a different path than settling back into being a Moisture farmer and swapping old rebellion stories at the Mos Eisley Cantina.

Building Character

You can learn the writer's lines, know the difference between down stage and up, have complete control over your props, figure out how to lay down the makeup to produce a black eye, and have mastered how to tie a bowtie onstage without a mirror. But all that work only produces a facsimile of a character . . . a picture that might be nice to look at but where does character lie? How can you trust this superficial person? Would you invest confidence in them? In order to walk the stage with confidence and speak with authority actors need to know more about the character they are portraying than what the playwright tells them. The writer may tell you what the character's name is . . . but other than that there really isn't anything much more there. It is up to you to dig as deep as possible into the when, who, what, where, and how that brings this role into the moment when the stage lights hit you in the face.

Here's a great exercise that I encourage every actor I've worked with to utilize in order to help find their character's inner life:

Make a list of the things your character might carry on their body, in a pocket, purse or backpack, in a wallet, or even just on hand on a daily basis. For example, (and for the purpose of this telling) these could be; a cell phone, a pocket knife, a change purse, a cross on a thin chain worn around the neck and a folded photo of young girl on a swing tucked into a wallet.

Realized each item carries weight. A conscious choice is made every morning to make sure that every item is picked up and carried out the door and into the world. Why that pocket knife? Perhaps it was one the character's grandfather carried with him religiously. Your character uses it to keep their fingernails clean through-out the day and overtime when they touch it they subconsciously think "Puppa." Perhaps this obsessive nail cleaning becomes a character trait and is organically absorbed into action during the course of the play.

So, think of each item as a metaphor that points to something deeper. Maybe stylish eyeglasses point to how your character feels about an insecurity they harbor over a scar just hidden behind thick frames. A scar that was inflicted by a schoolyard bully. That was inflicted when you, as the character, decided that you had had enough and finally fought back, ending the fear that they thrust upon you. It was your first victory in that life.

As you can see this simple exercise can quic your character a history that goes far beyond what the playwright envisioned or has given you. It is a story that now has roots in flesh and bone and blood. This skeleton doesn't need to be shared with anyone, director included. It is your personal story driven by your analysis of script. That said, the director and fellow cast members might offer you suggestions that will expand or perhaps change that story. Again, I urge actors to take the next step and keep a journal, written by the character, flowing through you from head and heart to arm, to hand, to pen. This journal can be remembrances, and/or just biographical. It can be poems composed, drawings made, or songs sung. It is uniquely yours. We all have a secret life. Things we keep to ourselves. That we don't share with life partners or family. Your character has these hidden locks (and keys) stashed away, that could be taken out and examined now and again. Or kept in darkness, kept secret even from them(our)selves. In fact they could lead to discoveries made during the course of the performance. A literal key worn as a necklace, that unlocks a metaphorical secret unknown to the character at the beginning of the play. An opening lock that is the revealing moment to a change the character goes through before the final curtain.

I specifically chose the Star Wars reference at the start of this chapter because it exemplifies this type of deep character work. In the Star Wars mythos Jedi knights built their own light saber. And the crystals that powered the weapon are found on a planet called Ilum. Each Jedi would go on a "vision quest" to gather a kybar crystal that would be incorporated into their saber. This became more than just a handy tool to have on you to deflect the occasional blaster shot. It held great emotional weight and in a Jedi's hand it gave the bearer authority and clout.

The backstory that you create is the Kybar crystal by which you gain both confidence in your choices and trust in the way your character moves through their world. Taking a backstory to this level gives the actor a significance that can make them a conquering hero. Skywalker of the Stage, so to speak, wielding a saber that cuts through fear.

Speaking of moving through the world. We all carry ourselves in an unique way. The physicalization of your character is another tool that you must become adept at falling into as you move from the wings to the stage. Shakespeare's Richard III comes to mind and if you have the opportunity I encourage you to find and watch the documentary film, "Now - In the Wings of the World Stage." It follows actor Kevin Spacey and company as they create and tour a production of Richard III. It shows how important it was to Spacey that he conquer the physical challenges the playwright presents via disability. As well as how those physicalizations affect the emotional landscape that Spacey, travels as Richard.

I, that am curtail'd of this fair proportion, Cheated of feature by dissembling nature, Deformed, unfinish'd, sent before my time into this breathing world, scarce half made up, And that so lamely and unfashionable that dogs bark at me as I halt by them;

Here is an exercise that works on your character's manner of taking space in the world:

- Speak the name of your character aloud. (For the purposes of this example we will call the character in question "Sue"). Think about the problems Su‹ the play. Think about the issues she faces and ‹ make her really tense. Where does Sue put that tension and how is it different of where you would find it in your own body.

- Exaggerate the tension you feel. Hold on to the area of the body that contains that tension.

Walk around the room. The tension you feel, thinking about what Sue has to face, should be so crippling that it's almost impossible to walk. It's so bad, Sue needs to come up with a way to get rid of it.

- How would you get rid of this tension? What do you do to get that tension out? Come up with an action and a sound that Sue does to get rid of tension. Make it big and make it loud - that's the only way to get rid of the tension. Let go.

Sue is now tension-free. Walk her around the room feeling good about herself.

- How does Sue walk? How does Sue's shoulders move? Do she bounce? Is she grounded? What does she do with her hands? - how is Sue different from "you."

Pretend Sue is walking down the street. Greet the first person she come into eye contact with. Make this person another character in the play

- Make sure Sue is reacting to them based on her relationship to them in the play. Are you close? Friends? Teacher/student? Talk to this person. Tell them where you're going and why you're walking down the street.

- Say goodbye to them. You have to be on your way. Greet another person. Repeat the process. Tell them where you're going and why. Say goodbye to them. You have to be on your way. Come to a neutral standing position.

- What is the most important line to you as the character in the play? What is the line that defines Sue? Close your eyes and think about what line you will choose.

When you have a line - Say that line out loud. Say it again. Yell it. Whisper it. Laugh it. Be angry with it. Be depressed with it. Choose an emotion you may use in the play.

- Now think about an action that goes with this line. And if Sue was unable to speak, what physical action would define this line? Be risky - does she roll into a ball? Does she skip? Reach up to the sky? Do yoga? Kick? This is not just some random action, this is an action that represents the most important line, which represents Sue. Is the emotion of the line coming out in the action?

Do the action and say the line at the same time. Do it again.

- And again.

Now, instead of saying the line, instead of saying words, come up with a sound. Again, it's a sound that represents the line, which represents Sue. Is it a yell? A note? A hum? A grunt? A groan? Don't use any words. Just sound. What's the emotional quality of the line? Of the action? What sound matches that emotional quality?

- Say the line, again. Now do just the sound. No action. Do it. And again.

Now do both the sound and the action. Put your heart into it. Commit to it.

- Come to center - Pat yourself on the back for finding more about your character than you realized you knew.

Alas, I have no idea where this particular exercise came from. Just a tool I had gathered and had stocked into my toolbox. I advise everyone to collect a set of wrenches and not to be shy about testing out a new one now and again. A fantastic thing that America has delivered to actors are Malls. If you have one at your disposal please spend a few hours there just watching people move. How they hold their bodies. What their gait is like. Do they slouch or stand stiffly erect? They have tension. Where have they stuffed it? Do you see your character? Where is Sue? Spot her and discretely follow her. Watch her shop . . . sit and drink coffee . . . carry purchases. If she becomes aware of you either explain yourself and apologize for unsettling her, or simply go on your way. But I urge you to consider the former over the latter. It is, of course, the riskier choice but you may also observe how she releases tension as she is reassured that you are not a stalker. Regardless, now try to incorporate the pay-off into your work. Take those unconscious physical mannerisms and make them your own . . . put them into your muscle memory bank until they are second nature.

So our saber now has a power cell heart and a hand grip but where is that unique sound that it is emitted when you flip the 'on' switch . . . bzuhzzzzzzzuhzzzzzuhzzzz.

Again backstory can be the key to unlocking your vocal cords. Suppose you are cast in a play written in the early 1900s that is being revived. Entitled "A Kentucky Belle", the role is that of Col. Wm McMillen described by the author as "a suitor." That's all we are given - however the dialogue proceeding his entrance lets us know that he is "remarkably rich" . . . followed by another character referring to him as "remarkably ugly, stupid and deaf."

Now it is known that the Carolina states and Kentucky were heavily settled by both Irish and Scots, so we can surmise, and perhaps make our first bold choice with this info. Since he is well off, he is more than likely 'old money' and his family has been in Kentucky for some time. That, along with the Mc in front of his name and the tidbit of info mentioned above, one can be reasonably certain he is of probable Scottish ancestry. Accent? Great place to start. But that accent has been tempered over time so just a 'hint' may be left in a way that can bring complexity and depth to the role.

It is known that American Bluegrass music was infused from its earliest days with Celtic musical traditions. Listening to older recordings of early bluegrass you can start to get a feeling for the cadence and meter that an old Scot gentleman from Kentucky might inherently use and sound like.

Is he as ugly, stupid and deaf as the other characters refer? Or are they just casting aspersions? Perhaps that ugly/stupid/deaf characterization actually stems from a slight stutter that the character has worked for years to conquer. Or maybe it is just envy. New money jealous of old.

Obviously the director of the play will have some

guidance here but it is up to the actor to bring these ideas and choices to the process. Why? Why spend all this time and work to paint such a detailed portrait? Because you want a fully functional weapon you can depend on and trust to carry you through any and all situations that will present itself to you. Such a detailed and strong foundation will make the saber battle of securing the role, of learning the script, of struggling to find the character, of taking final curtain bow a battle easily won. That carefully constructed, hand built lightsaber will crackle as you use it to cut a path across the playwright's world as it is put before an audience.

Here are a few nice little exercises to get your creative juices flowing as well as a bit of a recap for you:

What is the character's full name? Scripts and Playwrights might simply refer to a character as "Walter" or "Henrietta." What is the character's full, including middle, name?

How about family? Mother, alive or dead? Sisters ? Brothers? Favorite auntie? What makes you laugh? What makes you mad? Favorite Food? Least Favorite Food? Describe a childhood memory. Describe where you sleep.

All the above can go into a written journal that you are compiling as a part of your character development.

Grab a partner and rehearse a scene while doing a complex task. Solve a Rubic's Cube. Spread out a jigsaw puzzle and have at it. Start a pillow fight while you run a scene's lines.

Look beyond the obvious . . . Costuming and Makeup are the obvious. Set however? Most actors don't even give a second thought to a sofa on stage. But I always find objects on stage to invest in. Is this your living room? Where did you purchase that sofa? Was it delivered or did you have to drag it up five flights of stair breaking one of the sofa legs in the process. Making the set a part of your backstory and you will then have an actor's comfort in that space. Or a character's uncomfortableness . . . In William Mastrosimone's "The Woolgatherer", Rose invites Cliff back to her small one room apartment for a one night stand. The claustrophobic space is comforting for Rose but Cliff finds it unsettling. He is a man of the open road, while she seeks shelter from the raging storm of her psyche. For her, the small studio apartment is a womb . . . for him, a tomb.

Google Images can be a great tool for opening yourself up to what your character and their world may look like . . . A photo of a remembered childhood or a yet to become senior. Much like going to the mall and researching movement . . . Google Images can be a great tool for observations of a world outside the confines of the playwright's and your world. Art, Portraits, Posters and Art Photography can also inspire you and your imagination. And finally, just for giggles, cross gender cast the role in your mind. I was involved in a production wherein the script called for three males. The director chose to cast two females and one male. Unexpected and daring but it opened the production and the actors to completely new interruptions of the characters. Imagine Sam Shepard's True West with women in the roles of Austin, Lee and Saul. Imagine how different each character's backstory would have to be from one another simply because of the gender switch and where similarities lie. Opening yourself up to this sort of analysis will reveal choices that might otherwise lie hidden.

Finally, always examine the opposite of what your character is (or seems to be) saying. As you do your initial work with the script you will start to make obvious choices. But that can create expectations and eventual complacency. Trust your instincts but question the authority of your knee jerk judgments. There is always 'Terra Nova' hidden deep beneath the obvious landscape. And one must always be open to new "aha" moments even after you think you mastered the role. A stage Jedi takes nothing for granted and keeps is saber handy.

Chapter Five - It's not about you . . . it's about them.

Theater is, if nothing else, a grand piece of art created by a band of monkeys.

The Rehearsal

First and foremost the space in which you come together as a cast has to be a safe place. A place where play and work are encouraged and synergized. This should be where the Director takes the lead, with support from everyone in the room. Depending upon the particular production you may find not only a stage manager in attendance but if you are really really lucky, the playwright. If that doesn't terrify you then I need to reach out from the pages of this book grab you by the shoulders and shake. Wait a minute. Wait a minute. I would never do that. I'm just trying to grab your attention not your body. But speaking a writer's words and embodying a character that has, until now, existed only in the playwright's imagination can be a daunting experience. For all involved. This is an experience where one artist absolutely will sit in judgment of the spoken words and actionable deeds of another.

However truth will out, speaking as a playwright, this author is never judging the actor, rather their own work and self. Just as it is human nature for the actor to judge their own performance, the writer is much more interested in the battle they are fighting with their own inner critic. Self-analyzing of their script by the playwright is a given. Does it need work? Is it too 'talky'? Are plot holes crying out for an explanation? Where does the play sputter? And where does it soar too high and too soon?

The Director also is (or should be) more concerned with the ebb and flow of the action . . . the developing relationships between characters . . . and the comfort level in the space of all participants in trusting that freedom of expression is allowed.

The people we call designers, musicians, producers and all others may find their way into the rehearsal space - which could potentially cause a less than confident actor to become self conscious or closed down. Stop seeing these invited auditors as potential critics and start viewing them as compatriots. See them for what they are, collaborators and resources that can provide rich opportunity for an actor to enrich their own artistry. As I said before, if you want to play with the big dogs you have to get off he porch. If you want to BE a big dog you have to stay in the yard and PLAY with the BIG DOGS.

Much of the work that has been outlined in the preceding hasn't been done yet so that foundation of confidence isn't really there yet. So where does the mortar and brick come from? What tool is at your disposal to transform you from a yippy little ankle biter to a Rottiwiller who just wants to chase the ball? It's here. It is in realizing that all those former scattered back alley curs are actually a pack. The sooner that one accepts that each of you has the back of the other, the sooner that truth becomes reality. An actor who walks into first table read with that willingness to risk trust has already fetched the ball and brought it back without waiting for the toss. Actors who need to be coaxed along and need to sniff out everyone else's behind first are only serving to slow the process of "play" down to the speed of a kitten lying on its back and casually batting at a ball on the end of string. Be a Doberman. Show those lazy puppies that it is okay to run and fetch with abandon. Let your joyousness at diving into a pool to get that frisbee become infectious.

You know I keep yelling THERE ARE NO MISTAKES IN THEATER at you. But here . . . in the rehearsal hall . . . is exactly the place where "mistakes" are not only wanted but completely permissible. Not only wanted and permissible but enthusiastically encouraged! I once took on the chore of being an assistant director for a young writer who was directing his own work. And then watched him beat his cast into submission with line reading after line reading rehearsal after rehearsal. Demanding that each actor conform to some idea of how his puppets should behave. It was not only demoralizing to them, but limited their performances to lifeless boring mehs. The young director soon became confused as to why his playwright's play wasn't "working" as he envisioned it when he was being composing it on the page. There came an evening when the young playwright/director had a conflict in his schedule and was forced to turn rehearsal over to his assistant. We were far enough along in the process to be running acts and it fell to me to put everyone through Act I that evening in his absence. As he was putting on his coat and gathering up his belongings to head off he turned to me and admonished me "Do not change a THING!" "Oh of course not," I somewhat slyly replied. Once he was gone and the cast had done warmups and centered themselves, we gathered. I asked them to . . . cut loose. BE melodramatic. If you had made a decision to approach a line seriously, take an opportunity to find something hilariously funny instead. Do the opposite. Anything goes was the way we were going to work that evening. Needless to say they had a blast. And they simply would not let Act II be left to another day. We tore through the entire play like dogs ripping a soft-stuffed toy to pieces and fluff. When the last line was said and the imagined house lights raised, I only had one note for everyone. Go back to the way the director wanted it done. But bring to it anything and everything you may have discovered from that amazingly whack rehearsal. The next night our esteemed playwright turned director was back in his chair behind his table with his fat three ring binder script in front of him. Act II was open in front of him and his minions took the stage. It was the 'same' as the last time he saw it . . . but dramatically different. There was an energy that wasn't there before. He couldn't put his finger on it but somehow during the course of 24 hours his play had come alive as if struck by the lighting coming down on the towers of Doc Frankenstein's lab. Of course it slowly dawned on him that I had fiddled with some knob or switch on the bank of levers and gauges that made up his control panel. But in actuality I had little or nothing to do with it . . . other than to let the cat in our bag, out. I gave everyone permission to do anything and everything to that poor feline. They couldn't make a mistake in my rehearsal and they were now freed to cut loose within the confines that had been put in place around them by the playwright/director. They may have been still walled in . . . but now they at least had windows.

So, directors, well . . . are difficult to call 'trustworthy' and hardly worth being included in the spirit de corps that should be forged when everyone is trying to gain a foothold on that shear rock face of unknown territory needing to be exposed and explored. What to do when presented with a "challenging role" and you've tied your static rope to a challenging Lead Climber at the pinnacle? Well, first of all let's take a look at what I like to define as ***"Directing is tyranny masquerading as democracy."***

Here are five archetypical directors you may encounter during your travels across the stage.

#1 The Analyst

"What does it all mean"

Usually the first week(s) is devoted to table work and a somewhat arduous process of stripping the script to the bone. Working with a dramaturg to go into deep textual analysis and finding conflict(s). They demand a tight examination of character motivations and how each affects the world of the play.

How does this serve the play?

Total immersion into the work and world of the playwright will make certain the world the writer has created is realized. It also helps actors understand and create backstory. And deeper understanding of the whole picture is exposed as well. The actors can use this work once they are on their feet to bring clarity to the audience. It can also aid in line memorization and blocking motivation.

The danger is that the cast in general can lose a sense of cohesiveness by going off into their own little world(s) rather than living in the world of the play.

#2 The Dictator

"Do As I Say"

This type of director has a very specific (and occasionally narrow) view of how the process will unfold; they're not looking for input. Rehearsals are well-defined, blocking is well thought-out, the vision is tightly managed. The actor in the dictator-directed show does not usually get a lot of opportunity to offer suggestions or changes.

How does this serve the play?

Sometimes a production needs specific and narrow direction. And/or when you're working under tight time lines - specific and narrow direction is a necessity. In this context, "dictator" doesn't necessarily mean cruel or callous. Having said that, I'm never fond of the "no input at any time from anyone" scenario. This does not foster collaboration and artistic freedom.

#3 The Improviser

"Let's Make It Up Together!"

This director often comes to rehearsal with little to no blocking, few notes, but a lot of ideas. They are keen on collaborating with the cast. They improvise scenes between characters, have actors improvise blocking, and use plenty of exercises. Everything evolves and changes over the course of rehearsal. The input and involvement of the actor is key and necessary to the success of the Improviser Director.

How does this serve the play?

Usually it leads into or transitions into something more structured. It can be a thrilling experience for actor and director, as everyone works together in the creative process. I've been in amazing productions as an actor that utilizes this process. Everyone does need to be on the same page and willing to do the same amount of work. It is the director's job to make sure this happens and step in with a heavier dictatorial hand if and when needed.

If the director can't corral the creativity and move things along toward a cohesive product things can get messy. Without this oversight of the process the rehearsal can run in circles and no one gets the help needed.

#4 The Visionary

"Let's be creative, but I'm the boss."

This type of director enjoys the creative process, wants to hear from actors but ultimately is the one in control of the production. The best types of Visionaries are able to effectively communicate their vision and bring everyone on board, so they don't have to "be bossy." Everyone moves toward the director's vision on their own steam. They can bring their own ideas that serve the big picture that has been sketched out for them.

How does this serve the play?

Creativity within a structure can be amazing. Problems usually occur when the director is inconsistent. You can't ask for input from actors, then shut them off and refuse to implement their ideas. It's a fast way to lose the actors' trust. Problems can also happen when the director is wishy-washy in their communication of the vision.

An actor can't create effectively within a vision if they don't fully understand it.

#5 The Pusher

"Fight me!"

This type of director thrives on confrontation. They feel, rightly or wrongly, that the only way to get the right reaction out of a character is to push the actor. This can happen in a positive manner through question and discussion. The best Pusher doesn't mind when an actor disagrees or when an actor pushes back. But unfortunately, Pushers can stretch the emotions too far. And boundaries, if not set at the onset, can be quickly crossed.

How does this serve the play?

There's nothing wrong with encouraging an actor to move beyond their comfort zone. There's also nothing wrong with debate and conversation over a character, or a moment. That can be an exciting part of the process. But to push an actor emotionally just to get a certain type reaction out of performance? Completely hurtful, unnecessary and perhaps even harmful.

My advice is to talk with the Producer and/or Stage Manager if you feel a Director has crossed unexpected boundaries. Do not just "let it go." It is important to all involved that these types of conflict be dealt with in an open manner.

How do I (the author/director) work?

The approach that I most often take is a combination of the five. I tend to start off as an Analyst/Improviser . . .then mix in Visionary . . . as we get into the final weeks of rehearsal shift again into a Dictator/Pusher. I do try to set up this expectation at the first rehearsal so that everyone involved knows how the process will proceed and will not be blindsided by any of the above five archetypes. Hopefully, if I correctly set up a clarity and 'my door is always open' policy, no one (myself included) will feel compelled to create an agenda that doesn't serve the production, playwright, cast or crew.

What is any Director's responsibility?

Communication - working with a cast and crew is bringing a diverse group of artists together to reach a common goal. A "good" director will build a common lexicon or dictionary for all to use and understand. This lexicon should be different for every production and perhaps unique to the individuals involved. This allows everyone to come onboard with a shared vision. Actors should be kept in the loop on the design process as well. Seeing a model of the set or costume sketches will help everyone understand the end game and they will be able to invest in the world that they will inhabit. A good director will also understand individual actors may need more discussion that another.

So the question begs asking . . . What are some "bad" directorial choices?

- Give line readings - often a director will be tempted to fall into this shortcut - but it robs you of your own voice and short circuits the discovery process.

- Unannounced open rehearsals and allowing actors to give other actors notes. The "Dictator" needs to step up to the plate if comments are coming into the fray that are inappropriate to the process.

- Carelessness with the actors' time. Your call sheet should be adhered to and you shouldn't be standing around waiting. It is simply inconsiderate. That said, there is a reason tech week is called 'hell' week. Here your stage manager is your friend and should be able to lord over a director, demanding they remain respectful of the expectations they have set for you and the cast/production team.

- Standing on a pedestal. An unapproachable director who doesn't see themselves as a part of the process is death to the process. True artists view other artists as equals without judgment.

"A leader is best when people barely know he exists, when his work is done, his aim fulfilled, they will say: we did it ourselves." Lao Tzu

Obversely what are some “bad” cast/actor choices?

- Disrespecting the Stage Manager. Are you flipping crazy!? The stage manager is the closest you are going to get to meeting god in the flesh. And less I not mention it, disrespecting the tech crew. Tell a light board operator that they aren’t doing their job correctly and you will find yourself speaking the speech trippingly in the dark

- Showing up five minutes after “Call.” Now you are not only disrespecting the Stage Manager, but the rest of the production staff and your cast-mates as well. Make this your personal rule in life . . . Call is ALWAYS five minutes before Call.

- Ad libs and jokes. Put this in the ‘disrespect’ file drawer as well. Fast and loose doesn’t serve the audience . . . the playwright . . . or your fellow actors. Stick to the script. Execute the work. There is a difference between “Input” and “Insult.”

- Giving “advice” to other actors. Excuse me but this especially, IS NOT YOUR JOB. Not only do you run the risk of derailing the work of that a fellow actor but (here’s that word again) but disrespecting the director. Never ever never ever tell another actor how to play their role.

- Talking back stage. Voices carry as do whispers. If you think that “they” can’t hear you, guess again, they can. This is just as true in rehearsal as in performance. Focus on your own work and the work being done in your presence. Not in a scene? Use the time to get off book.

- And while we are on the subject . . . NO FOOD IN THE THEATER. Yes, you may have had to stop and grab a 7-11 sandwich so that you could be five minutes prior to call but respect the sacred space in which your art is created. Eat on the on the other side of the stage door. Not in the house, not on stage, not in the dressing room, not in the green room. (See Chapter 7)

- No Food ? No Smoking! No Vaping! No Alcohol! Again, take all that to the other side of the stage door. Such things are distractions from focus, confidence and trust.

-

Chapter Six - It's not about them . . . it's about you.

First these two messages from our sponsors -

A Cracked Pot *by Sacinandana Swami*

A Sunni water bearer named Vikram had two large pots, each hung on one end of the pole he carried across the back of his neck. One of the pots had a crack in it, while the other pot was perfect and always delivered a full portion of water at the end of the long walk from the stream, the cracked pot arrived only half full. This went on every day for two years, with the Vikram delivering only one and a half pots of water to his master's house.

Of course, the perfect pot was proud of its accomplishment and vainly saw itself as perfectly suited for the purpose for which it was made. But the poor cracked pot was ashamed of its imperfection and miserable that it was able to accomplish only half of what it had been made to do. After two years of what it perceived as bitter failure, it spoke to the Vikram one day by the stream. *"I am ashamed of myself and I want to apologize to you."*

"Why?" asked Vikram. *"What are you ashamed of?"*

"For the past two years, I have been able to deliver only half my load because this crack in my side causes water to leak out all the way back to the house. Because of my flaws you have to work without getting the full value of your efforts," the pot said.

Vikram felt sorry for the old cracked pot, and out of compassion he said, *"As we return to the house, I want you to notice the beautiful flowers along the path."* Indeed, as they went up the hill, the old cracked pot took notice of the sun warming the wildflowers on the side of the path. The pot felt cheered.

But at the end of the trail, the pot still felt bad because it had once again leaked out half its load, and again it apologized for its failure. Vikram said to the pot, *"Did you notice that there were flowers only on your side of your path, but not on the other pot's side? That's because I knew about what you call your "flaw" and took advantage of it. I planted flower seeds on your side of the path, and every day while we walk back from the stream, you've watered them for me. For two years I have been able to pick these beautiful flowers to decorate my table. If you were not just the way you are, I would not have such beauty to grace my home."*

Moral: Each one of us is unique, with perfect flaws—we are all cracked pots. But a compassionate, non-judgmental heart sees the perfection in our design. Viewing that unique beauty as talent despite any real or imagined defects.

Wabi-sabi: a new way to look at your whole life *by Robyn Griggs Lawrence.*

According to Japanese legend, a young man named Sen no Rikyu sought to learn the elaborate set of customs known as the Way of Tea. He went to tea-master Takeeno Joo, who tested the younger man by asking him to tend a garden. Rikyu cleaned up debris and raked the ground until it was perfect, then scrutinized the immaculate garden. Before presenting his work to the master, he shook a cherry tree, causing a few flowers to spill randomly onto the ground.

The Japanese revere Rikyu as one who understood to his very core a deep cultural thread known as ***wabi-sabi***. Emerging in the 15th century as a reaction to the prevailing aesthetic of lavishness, ornamentation, and rich materials, *wabi-sabi* is the art of finding beauty in imperfection and profundity in earthiness, of revering_authenticity above all. In Japan, the concept is now so deeply ingrained that it's difficult to explain to Westerners; no direct translation exists.

But broadly, *wabi-sabi* is everything that today's sleek, mass-produced, technology-saturated culture isn't. It's flea markets, not shopping malls; aged wood, not swank floor coverings; one single morning glory, not a dozen red roses. *Wabi-sabi* understands the tender, raw beauty of a gray December landscape and the aching elegance of an abandoned building or shed. It celebrates cracks and crevices and all the other marks that time and weather and use leave behind. To discover wabi-sabi is to see the singular beauty in something that at first look may seem decrepit and ugly . . . but with a deeper study reveals an inner, honest grandeur.

I wanted to start this chapter with the above two stories in order to really bring home the concept of opening yourself up to a new way of looking at your work . . . the world . . . and perhaps even your own life. Too many of us spend way too much time thinking that we are not good enough . . . or that some so and so is so much better than we are. This constant comparison to an ideal and idol doesn't serve us as artists. Every artist needs to come to a place of acceptance that the act of creation in and of itself is worthy of the applause that comes when the curtain call cue is called.

Where lies the actor's responsibility?

First and foremost – communication. For example, if you do not understand a specific note, ask. There are no stupid questions. It takes time to come to a common vocabulary between actor and director. The need for understanding outweighs what you might judge to be an embarrassing lack of knowledge about process. More than likely it isn't anyways. Participate and contribute actively to the creative process with suggestions. However - understand it is NOT your role to tell other actors how to approach their work. Yes, I said this before but it bears repetition. Own your own risk. Challenge yourself. Show up ready to work. This means ready to work at call time. Trust the process that is laid out for you. Commit. Respect. Have the back of your compatriots who are joining with you on your adventure.

I can not tell you the number of times I have asked actors to give me any and all potential schedule conflicts at the beginning of the process only to cast them and find out about too numerous to deal with conflicts. Any potential absences can be dealt with by the Stage Manager from the get-go if they are clearly outlined from the start. On my audition form, it is a question stated clearly up front as the commitment to the project needs to be understood even before casting. Both by the production team and by you. If this hasn't been done or something has changed in your time availability then do it at the first read through so that any issue can be worked out in a timely manner with the SM.

The actor's process in rehearsals.

Don't move, talk, or act until you have a clear intention and you're filled with a compelling emotion. - Alan Arkin

Warm up - not just movement and voice but centering and relaxation. Leave personal agendas at the door. Find a willingness to play, risk and experiment especially if you are feeling off or unfocused that day. Get over yourself.

GET OFF BOOK! The sooner that you can work without a script in your hand the sooner you can WORK. Break down the play by scenes. If you learn lines solely within the context of the play or only know the lines by virtual of blocking you are inviting fear. The same is true if you get into a very specific rhythm or only know the line before and the line after. What if another actor blanks? Or changes their blocking? Or says the line from three pages ahead? If you are so dependent on a certain cadence or on everything going perfectly, then you are printing up a blueprint for disaster. Get out of the habit of just learning lines by rote. Rather consider drawing your lines from a place of understanding the story being told from a deeper visceral level. Who am I talking to? What do I want? What roadblocks are being built in front of me? You should learn to nail down your lines by knowing what you want - and - what you need - and - how you are going to get it - and - how your character interacts with scene partners - and - what story are you telling. This isn't saying you don't need to know your cue lines or should endeavor to learn your scripted part exactly as the playwright presents it for you. That is, of course, your primary job as an actor BUT, with as much depth as possible, know the story that is being told through the eyes of your character. If the playwright has done their job then the lines should almost flow organically out of that.

Making the most of your rehearsal.

- Control the other person's attention. As a matter of fact DEMAND it.
- Breathe. Connect breathe. Oxygenate. Get comfortable with your diaphragm. You are going to need it
- Be open and honest in moment to moment.
- Allow creativity. Allow? Give free reign.
- Seek the unexpected, not the expected. Surprise yourself.
- Risk.

Prepare for rehearsal in advance by studying the scene(s) on your call sheet. Look at a scene in detail. Run the script. Go through it line by line. Ask yourself questions about the scene, about your character. Make sure you know any background information that comes up in the scene, that you're clear on the relationships with the other characters in the scene. Uncertain? Ask! In other words . . . what is the story that the playwright is telling here and what is my part in that story?

Then after you, your scene partners and the director have set blocking, review the script. Now is the time to nail down your lines, while the work is still fresh in your head. At the risk of repeating myself . . . understand the story of the scene. In every moment your job on stage is not "what's my next line?" but rather "what is happening to me?" And, of course, "How do I manipulate this situation to get what I want?" Then throw your script away (just jesting - that's where all the notes you take during rehearsal are located).

Do or do not. There is no try. Yoda

Prop familiarity. Make sure that you become as familiar as possible with the props that you will be using during the process. While you may not have the "dress" prop to work with you can substitute it with a similar object. Think about the everyday items that litter your life. If you have a favorite gold colored yo-yo that you use to divest yourself of nervous energy, you don't have to figure out how to walk the dog. You mastered that trick the first week you had the thing. It has a familiarity that is comfortably gained from everyday use. Props should be that familiar. Perhaps more importantly . . . invest in a secret object or prop that only you and your character knows about. It doesn't necessarily have to be something that accompanies you onto the stage. It might be kept at your makeup station. Or it could be kept in a pocket but never produced. But it can contain your character's power and serve as a secret totem of it. Invest in that totem.

Tie blocking to motivation. Often a director will block to create "tableau." It is your job to figure out how to tie blocking to organic specific movement. Remember the director has the "eye" of the audience. He or She has a view of the unfolding action from a view point that you cannot have or gain. I was fortunate enough to be able to sit on rehearsals conducted by the marvelous Maria Irene Fornes. She embodied the "Dictator" as a director and would demand "2 steps stage right **<u>not</u> 3**." Watching her work unfold in performance was like watch dance or seeing a living painting. Truly masterwork. I also saw actors puzzle over the why of "2 steps not 3." And then watched them change from puzzlement and potential frustration to trust and respect. Realizing that there is more work being done in rehearsal than just your own opens you up to becoming a part of an act of creation that is bigger than yourself. This is the webbing of a "safety net" worthy of the Big Top.

Work out your character's inner monologue. Seek "active" verbs that click like falling dominos in your head, even when you are simply sitting in a chair on set silently without speech. The audience will hear your thoughts and take note of your active engagement. If you have an honest inner monologue during these silent moments then your reactions to what you are observing will require no "acting" (or as is often the case, overacting). This is even more important when you are speaking. We are always thinking and plotting. The words that spill out of our mouths are constantly being composed mico-moments before utterance. Internally, we can be thinking something completely different than what we just said, sometimes thinking the opposite of what we are saying as we are saying it. Those are powerful character attributes that make you compelling on stage. An active ongoing inner monologue tied to character's needs, wants and desires will leave no room for self-judgment of the actor's work while the actor is onstage. Your inner monologue must be an integral part of the real life struggle your character is going through and that makes it riveting to observe.

Experiment - Look for surprises - Don't expect. Seek the Aha and EUREKA! Lay down challenges for yourself and your scene partner(s). This is one place risk is of primary importance and why I stress embracing fearless risk. Making each and every moment seemingly real is the external yin to the internal yang. Approaching your moment to moment life on stage as if it were rehearsed only shows the expected and complacent. To really be alive and put the audience on the edge of their proverbial seat requires that you embrace the idea that anything can happen next. Expect only the unexpected. This is why I suggest becoming so immersed in script that you literally can throw the book away on opening night. Not only should you no longer need it, you should no longer want it. This lies at the heart of fearless acting. Without the element of fear that "anything can happen next" running through-out your time on stage then the performance will be "meh." So you only achieve fearless acting by allowing yourself to be constantly fearful. Ironic eh?

Take notes. I am constantly amazed by actors who do NOT carry a pencil with them at all times during a rehearsal. Granted you cannot always make notations during the moment that you and the director are working . . . but you should find time to review your work and jot down discovery/blocking/beats etc in the script for future reference and review as soon as you can. As a director I always make certain to give actors the time to do exactly that and question them when I notice them not jotting things down. That question you had during the process will become forgotten by the time a discussion regarding the work takes place. And the answer to that question could be one that pushes the first domino over in your elaborate setup. I even encourage actors to stop me from moving forward until they have had a chance to jot "it" down. Now you have a reason to keep your script out of the trash can and close at hand.

What is the Rehearsal's Responsibility?

Discovery, discovery, discovery. As mentioned in the previous chapter . . . this is the place where you have complete freedom to make a complete fool out of yourself. If you do not feel comfortable and relaxed enough to try new approaches to the material then something is amiss. In rehearsal there is nothing but room for "too much" or "over the top." Make **Bold** choices . . . even if you end up setting any choice aside in favor of another later discovery, being bold in rehearsal will help you discover the uncovered territory. As mentioned above, if you pursue "safe" out of a desire to be free from the worry of fear, then the production and your work in particular. will be un-interesting and expected. In performance risk will ALWAYS produce a "fresh" show. As long as you are true to character and honest in your approach it will never be wrong. BOLD choices and remember (you are going to make me say it aren't you?) there are no mistakes in theater. Find safety in risk.

But, let's talk about the word "bold" for a moment as I am tossing it around here with abandon. Many of the actors that I have worked with assumed that to mean "loud" or "dramatic." But that isn't what defines a bold choice. A bold choice might be to whisper rather than shout. Or to sit absolutely still rather than leap. It may be a gentle approach to a reprimand when your first instinct might be harsh. So rather than prattling on about it assuming you know how I mean what can be a nebulous term. So let's take a second or two to really define it. It really is somewhat of a mishmash (hence nebulous) of a variety of things starting with . . . fearlessness. It is, perhaps, how and why I arrived at the title of this book. If you are making a choice that might make you slightly uncomfortable, then you are probably on the right track. Be brave cause as you know, there aren't any mistakes here especially in rehearsal. Innovative, ingenious and inventive. A fresh approach rather then falling back on old tricks that are tried and true for you is called for. And finally, specificity. Risk doesn't necessarily mean "random." In fact bold needs to be a "focused Fresnel" not a color wash. Know why this choice you are making is being made. Be able to defend it and stand behind it. That said (and here is where it gets tricky) don't go rogue. If your director is asking you to rethink your choice understand that they may have specific objectives that fit the larger picture that need to be brought into consideration. Your scene partners also need to be considered. Don't turn a choice into a two by four. Don't go wacky and whack someone upside the head. And then the playwright also needs consideration. The closer you are to the character's intent with your choice, the more honest that bold choice will be.

Rehearsal should be simply a means to provide a structure within which you can work. The space should provide the actors freedom of movement and the opportunity to create surprise (as suggested earlier, doing a scene throwing pillows at one another can invoke surprising discovery). The work accomplished here should not only encourage moment to moment astonishments but allow the actor to see that making risk possible will not destroy the work and, in truth, will elevate it.

As the rehearsals get closer to tech week choices will finalize. Clear intentions and motivations should be laid out as a part of the above mentioned framework. But this framework needs to be flexible enough to allow experimentation and change. Even during the performance part of the process an actor needs to be open to flexibility, both from themselves but also from others. The aforementioned Ms. Fornes also led me to accept that the rehearsal never really ends. You are just allowing the audience in to observe the ongoing pealing back of the layers of the artichoke that is a vital part of creating art and revealing truth.

So please take note if it isn't obvious that I do not view a production as a "product" but rather a process. It is not the actor's job to deliver a product, that belongs to the director and the designers and the crew. The actor's job is to create the unexpected within an expected environment. So, the bottom line for everyone working to unveil the writer's story, should be creating an environment where it is safe enough invite an audience in to watch the unanticipated. That is how they have their Ahas and Eurekas. Therein lies awakening joy or sadness, the catharsis embodied by the masks of comedy and/or tragedy.

Chapter Seven - Ritual, the art of creation. If you meet Buddha on the road - kill him

Thespian:

- A citizen of the ancient Greek city of Thespiae
- referring to Thespis of Icaria, the first credited actor (the first person ever to appear on stage as an actor playing a character in a play) Thespis is credited with the invention of theatrical touring; he would tour various cities while carrying his costumes, masks and other props in a horse-drawn wagon.

The term comes from a Greek word meaning "action" which is derived from the verb meaning "to do" or "to act."

We need to re-seize the term "Thespian." It describes someone who not only "acts" - but one who acts with the thoughtfulness that encompasses the history of storytelling. Somewhere in the midst of the twenty century the label became associated with theater nerds in high school. It needs to be reclaimed and be re-given the respect and reverence that comes from thousands of years of humans donning the masks of comedy and tragedy while on the boards.

Hopefully you can see that I am not using the words "reverence" and "respect" lightly here either. I view the physical theater . . . the backstage . . . scene shop . . . rehearsal rooms . . . the box office . . . the theater in its entirety as a "holy space." It's important to remember that theater the Greeks presented were plays about their gods and their relationship to humans. And the audience that sat in those amphitheaters didn't come to be entertained (though I am certain that they were), they came to have an emotional cathartic experience. Something that moved them passionately and incited fervor within. They expected to walk away changed men and women. If you attend a fundamentalist religious event you would get a taste of the way theater can move powerful emotions through the body and affect someone physically. Fire and brimstone preachers can knock true believers off their feet with the wave of a hand. These performances are perhaps the 21st Century equivalency of Greek theater, complete with “chorus."

Humans want desperately to have a personal relationship with something larger than themselves. I aver that we strive to "touch the creator" by being agents of creation. I often refer to my father who wanted me to pursue a career in law. He saw my natural love of speaking and theater as a vehicle to a high paying job. And he could never quite understand why I chose the life of an artist . . . chasing after a "dream" at the expense of shaky financial security. He was very much blue collar working class and of course wanted a white-collar upper middle class lifestyle for his son. Yet, when he retired he took up painting. And specifically water colors. He found the forgiving medium was the best way for him to tap into a way of expressing himself in a ways that he had never experienced before. But moreover he discovered what it was like to be "filled with the muse.” The experience of picking up a paintbrush and finding hours slip away un-noted filled him with wonder. It was when he came out of his first revelries enmeshed in the act of creating that he finally realized why his son made the choices that he did. There was a spiritual fulfillment that was unexpected and dare I say, rapturous. All actors should open themselves up to this experience. This is why roadblocks need to be identified and graded to a smooth surface. As I said earlier, you need to find a safe place to fill yourself with fear, and be fearless about it.

Stretching all the way back to painting pictures of aurochs on cave walls humans have told stories. Through the telling humans shared a bond beyond the physical. A tribal connection to one another through the experience of telling and listening. The teller reveals a deep part of self, the listeners reveal an enlightenment about how they perceive the world anew. This intimacy between teller and listener is a psychic connection. Both are involved in a creative process that neither may even be conscious of happening while it is transpiring. A process taking place in the moment "now" when the story is being told and received. It is malleable in that it can change depending on when, where and how the story is related. Each telling is a “new" experience - even if the same story is told.

Perhaps the flood story that many Westerners only know from the Old Testament of the Bible is a perfect example. It actually is a story told by many different cultures in different settings with different props and costumes. And I suspect this particular story goes back to a shared experience between a people that time and history has forgotten. But regardless of where told it gave humans (and perhaps still does) a connection with nature and something larger than themselves.

So I am not far off base when I describe the theater as a holy place. A church if you will. Where both actor and audience come together to create a new-shared creation experience for themselves through the art of a story told. The lights that cause shadows to flicker are really not that different from a stack of burning logs. And the pictures presented not that different from the rough paintings of hunters on a cave wall bringing down a wooly mammoth. Early on, my life in the theater was doing a traveling show with trunks that contained all our costumes and props. We presented sword and sorcery shows, as well as epic high sea adventures. I remember with crystal clarity a young audience member coming up to me after a show about pirates to ask a very important question. He wanted to know why . . . when I climbed back on board the Spanish Sea Galleon after being tossed overboard . . . why I wasn't wet. I was thunderstruck. Here we were presenting a pitched battle on the high seas with nothing more than a piece of cloth for a sail and a piece of wood with a wheel stuck on it . . . and his imagination filled in all the missing trappings. He literally created that large, multi-decked sailing ship, complete with rigging and plank. The power of his ability to create made me realize that what I was doing bottomless and profound. I never looked at the theater and my place in it in the same way again. From that moment on, every stage I ever set foot on was surrounded by a cathedral complete with soaring towers and gargoyles even if it was an abandoned warehouse basement or some place with a proscenium arch.

In that moment I knew that I was carrying forward a torch that went back tens of thousands of years. And had the potential to not only entertain, but enlighten. So is it any wonder that I place such a high value on "respect." This is why as an actor, one has a responsibility to the craft that needs to be approached with ritual. So far I've described many facets of that ritual. The carefully preparation of character . . . the rehearsal of the movements of the play (both physical and emotional) . . . the abandonment to both the risk and joy of playing in the moment.

No one can teach you how to act. It is something

anyone can do but few succeed at. By that I mean anyone can learn the lines, the blocking, put on the makeup, the costume, have the stage manager push them out onto the stage and not bump into the furniture. But can they do so with élan and conviction that doesn't betray the fact that they are a pretense of real? Therefore the question is then, when does the "action" in "acting" start?

The answer . . . and the secret is . . . (get out your pencil you might want to jot this down in the margins of the book) you don't need a script to act. Nor a set . . . or a character . . . or any of the things we've been discussing so far. What you REALLY need is imagination. You have to be open to not only being the storyteller with only their voice to paint a sunset, but you need to have the open imagination of a ten year old boy who wonders why that sailor didn't climb back on board dripping wet with seaweed caught in his beard. I understood that the real reason that kid didn't get to see my salty sea dog drenched was because I didn't BELIEVE that I was storm tossed. I was simply in costume, saying my lines . . . and doing what the director told me to do when I was supposed to do it. Rather, I should have been dripping in salt water spitting out a barnacle or two that came splashing in with that last gasp for air. I needed to commit fully to becoming the storyteller.

In this discovery I realized what was missing and how to take myself to the next level as an actor. I needed a ritual that would allow me to fully invest myself in not only my character, but place myself in that holy space of creation. I stopped treating the theater as a theater . . . and started to believe it to be a Notre-Dame of my imagination. I worked this meditation into my centering exercises that I did as a part of my warm-up prior to any rehearsal or performance. I would imagine my spiritual body expanding and filling every space large and small contained within the walls that made up the building. I centered around the collaboration that had taken place . . . and was about to happen in order to manifest a new creation. A story unique and never before experienced by anyone. Something rehearsed a thousand times but never before performed in that moment, at that altar, with that congregation.

Each actor will come up with a their own centering ritual. In one production a few years back I noticed that the actor sitting next to me at the makeup tables kept his brushes, powder, base, liner, rouge, comb and all the accouterments that one's kit contains - carefully and obsessively laid out in such exact detail that it bordered on compulsive. Yes, slightly disturbing and at first glance odd. But then I came to realize that this was his "ritual." It was how he brought everything together and centered his impending performance. I suppose I should also point out that this actor worn only red right down to his underwear and shoes. Red from hat to toe. So yeah, anal retentive and slightly annoying as well, but centered and reverent in his process.

How does this relate to Fearless Acting? Personally for me, this sort of zen ritual brings everything together long before the word "places" can be spoken by the stage manager. It was and is a way for me to embrace that concept of "something bigger than myself" and turn myself completely over to trusting the perfect wabi-sabi of any moment that is about to transpire. That wabi-sabi is completely acceptable and in fact called for. This broken pot holds precious water that is about to nurture sprouting flowers. It serves to remind me that my support system is all encompassing. My work, the work of my fellow actors, the work of the stage crew, the director and designers - and most importantly the audience - those who are anxiously waiting for the houselights to dim and the curtain to rise are all a part of the moment. All anxious for their opportunity to join in the act of creation. All anxious for that catharsis of either comedy or tragedy. Perhaps even a mixture of both. Ultimately I see that they are likely more anxious than I. Within this moment I find nothing but love for them and cannot wait to get things started with all the audacity and impudence I can fearlessly muster.

Chapter Eight - Stop Acting you're upsetting the children

Perhaps one of the easiest ways to get comfortable in the skin of being an actor is sitting right outside your front door. Go out into the community of your peers. See every thing that you can. Volunteer to usher at theaters if ticket prices are an issue for you (or even if they aren't, theaters NEED volunteers) and if your community has a fringe scene, grab a date and see something outside your normal realm of experience. Support what your friends are doing and if they have a friend in a show ask if you can tag along when they go to support that friend. Trust me, seeing everything you can pays off in the long run.

I came of age in the town of Ashland, Oregon, home to one of the largest Shakespeare festivals in the country. I worked as a waiter in one of the many restaurants in that tourist town and when my shift was over I would wander by the outdoor stage usually right around the time that the final act or acts were about to take place. I could usually slip quietly in and stand at the back of the house and observe. I took in everything from the actor's approach to the lines, to the set designer's staging to the director's blocking choices. I saw things that worked and things that didn't. I became friends with production and stage managers as well as box office staff and costume shop seamstresses . . . it was after all a small town . . . and more often than not I could snag a comp ticket to the any of shows running on their three stages. At that time, the festival also did, by invitation only, little shows at midnight . . . doing work that normally would not be seen on any of the mainstages. The time spent in this theater town . . . with access to this living museum . . . allowed me to absorb all aspects of the theater arts.

When I made the move to Seattle I sought out the people who are doing theater the way that I liked and doing what I wanted to do. Without hesitation I turned around and asked the artistic and managing directors at those venues how I could help. Because, as mentioned above, everybody needs help. As someone who managed a small fringe theater in the shadow of that big theater on the hill I knew the value of dedicated volunteers. And eventually I landed a gig as House Manager of New City Theater. Wow, what an opportunity. Over time I was able to spend time in the physical space people while they work. The artistic director allowed me to sit quietly in on rehearsals. I got to meet some movers and shakers of that world that normally I would have never have had the chance to meet let alone discuss process with. I met my wife there! In other words I did what I needed to do to get involved, then worked my way into positions that allowed me to grow. It was always amazing and the experience forged me.

So, speaking from personal experience, do not be shy in make people aware of you. Invite theater professionals to see whatever you may find yourself involved in. Reach out and ask if they might be interested in seeing your work no matter what the venue.. Offer them a comp ticket. These folks are usually deeply involved in their own production schedules and will more than likely not be able to come . . . unless you make it know to them that you want their input and sincerely value it. Because of their own commitments you can not expect them to show. They can be busy in their own world but if they do make the effort, gods forbid you forget to thank them for showing up and be sure to ask for their honest assessment of your work. I promise that they will remember you.

You must become aware of what is happening outside of your world. Read the plays that are being produced in your town and the next town over. Take notice of roles that speak to you and what you think you may be appropriate. Contact the theater that is producing that play. Tell them you'd like to be considered in future productions. Tell them politely you would love to audition for them. If they don't invite you to audition, or the show is already cast, or they ignore you completely, go and see the show anyways. See how they approach their art. Volunteer to usher!

Go to generals if and when they happen. Get to know other actors who are there waiting to be seen. Hang out after your audition, if possible, to see who walks in the door. If it's a situation where you can watch the auditions unfold, so much the better! Break the ice with those actors whose work you admire. When you go to shows and you see work you like, hang out afterwards by the stage door, introduce yourself and sincerely congratulate that cast member on their great work that moved you. Get to know your peers in your community. Network your ass off.

I moved up to Everett from Seattle after a long life in the theater scene in the Emerald City. In the past I rarely ventured that far north and knew basically no one and nothing about the work that was being done there. But quickly became aware of a company that was producing work at the Historic Everett Theater, an old restored vaudeville house. The A.D. was a gent named Scott Randall and he had a long relationship with the Historic and helmed a company called Red Curtain. We met over coffee and talked about my background and his. He gave me a tour of the theater and we began an association that continues to this day. I watched him move his base of operations from Everett to the next town over . . . where he is establishing an Arts Center that goes far beyond what either of us imagined way back when sitting talking over coffee. I mention this to make the point that a life in the theater never need end. When and if you move, start anew. Get yourself out and about. Build a new network. Risk again.

And if you find yourself un-cast, not in rehearsal, with the phone not ringing, and your email inbox is nothing but spam then for gods sake . . . MAKE YOUR OWN WORK. All that networking you've done! Get everyone together . . . do cold readings with one another. Find out what your professional peers want to do and then do it. When I lived in Ashland I wasn't classical trained and at that time I didn't think of myself as an actor who could handle the work demanded by iambic pentameter. So instead, with a few friends, we wrote swashbuckling adventures that involved a wide range of stage combat technique. We choreographed fights, wrote our plays around them and then took it on the road. We toured Southern Oregon and Northern California with props and costumes in a box and performed wherever we could find a platform that rose six inches off the floor (sometimes we didn't even have that) and enough room to swing a sword without damaging an audience member. It didn't cost alot and we worked our asses off. And this was where I discovered the meaning of this word Audacity. If I can do it you can too. If you have the drive and energy to make it happen then . . . Make. It. Happen. You do need that network and that is why I stress how important it is for you to not sit at home but to go out and discover who and what is going on around you.

After roaming the countryside I settled down in Ashland and made a new theater with a new network that produced work that wasn't being done at in Bill Shakespeare's house. We did contemporary modern plays. Albee, Shepard, Durang, Stoppard, Pinter, Shanley, Mamet. We found actors who were playing "the third spear carrier from the left" up at the Big House and let them cut loose directing that script that they always wanted to but wouldn't get to do up there. We found dishwashers and retail sales clerks who didn't get cast at the Big House but ended up hanging out in town anyways, and gave them the roles that weren't being presented to them anyways. Over the course of the years that I lived in that valley four other "fringe" companies sprung up around us producing some cutting edge stuff on a shoestring. In essence we proved that you can create art with tin can lights, a board made out of household dimmers and costumes found at Goodwill. And others followed.

So keep track of the artists you admire and then do not hesitate or be afraid to approach them and find out what kind of theater ignites their creative soul. Stay in touch with writers and directors whom you have come across. Ask them what they would love to tackle. Don't limit yourself to having a theater on which to stage your play. We often performed in bars and nightclubs with no expectation of recompense. Simply splitting the door with the owner and letting them sell as much alcohol and food as they could to a captive audience.

Become a wingman. I hooked up with a few folks who shared an obvious chemistry with me. Together we took on the world. In fact my wife and I literally forged a theater dedicated to producing new work out of nothing but imagining that it could be done. It ended up being one of the only theaters that was doing new work at that time. We showcased emerging talent. And wrote our own shows if nothing else was exciting us. Don't be afraid to let your partners shine. It will only reflect back on you in the most positive way.

And don't be reticent to ask for money. Shakespeare's company, The King's Men, did not make a living from ticket sales. They had a patron. One of those early fringe theater companies that I created with a pal of mine funded our entire season using donated props and costumes, salvaged lumber, back alley cast off set pieces and revenue from program ad sales. We bartered for printing in exchange for giveaway ticket blocks. We asked for large scale donations from corporations. We wrote grants seeking funding. And we got all the above and more. Networking.

Use 21st Century tools. On the web you can usually find online resources or a database calendar for theaters in your location. This calendar will show you all the rehearsals, performances and - most importantly – auditions happening in the area. So, if you happen to see auditions for, say, "Actor's Resident Theater of Winnemucca" on their website coming up in 2 weeks, you know that you should be sending off a resume and asking for a slot to the Artistic Director via e-mail NOW. (Who, by the way, saw you in Reno last year because you invited them.)

The point is . . . always be working. Even when you are not cast in a show, do any of the things mentioned above to keep your artistic life alive. And don't be so picky about what show you are choosing to audition for. Audition for everything. This not only helps you overcome the issue you may have with putting yourself on the line. It also will expand your range and give you the opportunity to put everything we have been sharing here into action. Even if it is a smaller role than what you want or working with a script that you may not have a full awareness of the value of, working in a stimulating fulfilling environment is far more important than landing that plum role, or worse yet sitting at home and watching old Law and Order episodes.

Above all - don't get complacent. Let's say you start work a lot. Your new-found comfort and confidence in auditioning is starting to pay off. Maybe you don't even have to audition anymore as "they" are calling you! And . . . you start phoning it in. In both rehearsal and performance. These are signs that you are losing respect for your craft. A painter may have a favorite brush - but if their brush bristles become rendered useless due to hard coats of paint or have lost their softness and original shape, then it is time for either repair or replace. You do NOT want to be replaced. There are thousands of others who would give up sitting and watching Law and Order SVU to be where you are. And don't assume that you are going to be aware of your complacency. You need to take long thoughtful looks into a mirror now and then. And I am not talking about the coated glass in your bathroom. Fresh perspective can come from many sources but are usually outside yourself. A good one is a critic's harsh review. Here you've been not judging yourself as I advise but now know that is a double-edged sword. While it can be a good thing that helps you not second guess your work . . . it also can blind you to that needed swift kick in the pants that you used to give yourself after self judging an audition. Here it becomes very apparent that work you have undertaken has fallen into product rather than process. Become aware again that you are not working on this play followed by the next, followed by the next. A singular production is just the medium, like a painter's canvas. You are the brush that brings the painting to life. In an essential way, you are constantly working on the soul of an artist, becoming the creator. Live the life of an artist. And I know you know what I mean since you read the last chapter to get here, so let's just leave it at that.

Getting back to standing in front of that mirror. Your work needs to be constantly held up in front as many mirrors as you can surround yourself with, not just one. In order to gain a fresh perspective on a continual basis you need harsh mirrors and loving mirrors, political mirrors and personal mirrors, male mirrors and female mirrors.

And where do these mirrors come from? Where else but the arts? Movies, music, dance and theater. Where else but life? Friendships, travel, commitment to social justice and love. Surround yourself with these metaphorical mirrors and, I promise you, everything's going to be more than OK, everything is going to be spectacular.

Chapter Nine - Get off the stage - Speaking in Public

So far I've focused on actors and acting in the theater. But anyone who gets up and stands before a group can and does find themselves with a constricting throat, shaking hands and a feeling of sinking slowly into quicksand. But everything outlined here can be directly related to any situation. A business person who is scheduled to present a slideshow at a meeting. A keynote speaker at a luncheon. A sales person giving product demonstrations at a trade show. A poet stepping up to the lectern at an open mike. An officiate at your sister's wedding. A celebrity host at an awards show. Anytime that anyone is in a position of being exposed in front of a group . . . stage audacity is waiting to happen. So let's look at applying everything we've discussed and try to apply it to these different situations. And by doing so, use this opportunity to review these techniques.

Have you already forgotten? No mistakes. The best example that I can think of is a recent political speech presented by Jeanine Pirro announcing her intent to run against then presidential candidate Hillary Clinton. Ms Pirro's speech went swimmingly. Until she abruptly stopped short and stood completely silent for what seemed to be minutes. It was actually about 30 seconds but 30 to 45 seconds of "dead air" on the stump can seem like a long long time. Both to the speaker and the audience. Finally in a muffled meek voice she turned and asked nearby staffers "Does anyone have page 10?" Needless to say the experience shook her and for the rest of the event she was befuddled and "off her game." The flub cost her the shot she wanted to take at the presidency. The lost page became the one thing anyone talked about when her name was mentioned.

So how could this public speaker have turned disaster into victory? First of all she was ill prepared. She didn't give due diligence prior to stepping up to the mike to "building a backstory" and "getting off book." According to an aide, her remarks were written just prior to going out. So instead of telling a story about her life, qualifications and what she had to offer . . . she was dependent on the sheets of paper in front of her on which she had quickly jotted down thoughts. Now don't get me wrong. Plenty of people keep crib notes in front of them or speak from a chapbook at an open mike poetry event. BUT, they, unlike Jeanine, put their confidence in knowing the prepared statements that they are about to give in rather than depending on Page Ten.

J.P. lacked a willingness to risk honestly. Think about it. If she had trusted in her audience's suspension of disbelief then she could have simply said something along the lines of . . . "I seem to be missing what I was about to say" or "Don't you hate it when that happens?" or "No matter - what I am speaking about doesn't require carefully crafted sound bites!" And simply forged ahead. Speaking off the cuff about the matters that were important enough to her to compel her to stand at the microphone and speak. She missed a huge opportunity for success because she wasn't willing to RISK. And risk with honesty in that exact moment. All of us have lost our train of thought and had to back-peddle a bit to get a conversation re-ignited. So her audience (which, since it was televised ended up being in the millions) would have instantly identified with her and been even more willing to have her back here. Instead she let her fear of risk shut her down completely turning her into the proverbial deer in headlights.

And then she allowed her inner critic to insist that she made a huge mistake and this in turn blurred her focus. She fell into the mistake of believing that she had made an irretrievable blunder. This blindside was like a crowbar to the side of her head and literally made her see stars and birdies. In turn this set up a cavalcade of missteps and wrong turns. She literally made herself a sight to be seen once she lost sight of her safe space. A memorable spectacle but not in a breathtakingly beautiful way.

Perhaps a better example for you would be the opposite of the above. A public speaker who maintains their confidence and composure when everything seems to be failing around them is Steve Jobs. He was wonderful to watch when he gave Keynote addresses during the launch of any new Apple product. As often is the case when dealing with tech and computer slide shows the planned presentation will stop dead in its tracks . . . or skip ahead a slide or the microphone will fail or countless other hiccups or technical errors that can and will happen along the way do. For someone who is using tech for their address a disaster scenario is potentially more embarrassing than walking out having forgotten your pants. But Steve was so confident in his material . . . so at ease with his audience . . . and possessive of a willingness to trust that nothing is actually going wrong even when everything was terribly amiss that you, as audience, never really noticed anything was going awry. These two particular cases, in contrast to one another, speak volumes.

Not only do I not have a script but my pants are gone

I've set aside improv till now as it's the one thing that truly terrifies me and I have a tendency to stay away from it. Partly because in my opinion to do it and do it well you need to find partners who have a dynamic chemistry that ebbs and flows quickly, naturally and effortlessly. Taking classes specifically in improv is one of the strongest ways to conquer standing in front of a crowd, large or small, without sweat, without script and without pants. The first fundamental is something that actors must do whenever they are on stage (and it is extremely easy to do) is active listening. Obviously if you are speaking alone this doesn't make to much sense at face value. After all you are alone on the podium. But think of it in the larger context of heightened awareness. You need to get out of your head and not let the next thing you have to say become the overwhelming focus. If you are concentrating so hard on what you are about to say then you're going to miss something really important. The awareness that you bring to your performance or presentation puts you in the present moment and makes your presentation compelling. The "moment" is always truly unique and special. Knowing that the moment is singular, forces you to quiet the mind and be present. You have no room to analyze or over-analyze. There is only time to just be.

When you work with a group in an improv situation there can be no judgment: anything goes, anything can happen. The crazier it is, the more you push forward. And it builds that support safety net that we discussed way back in chapter one out of steel cable. It becomes about group success. When the group succeeds, you succeed. The only way improv can work is if you leave your agenda at the door.

Remove ego from the equation and something awesome happens organically.

So if you find that you approach improv with reticence then how can you even think to participate? The only way to conquer fear is to embrace it. Hug it out and you will find that fear quickly turns on its head. You just have to take a deep breath and dive in. Cold water often is assumed to be frigid, but can actually be degrees more pleasing than you imagined it being. Don't be a tail tucked puppy. Jump in after that ball.

The simplest thing to hang onto is . . . and this is of particular importance in public speaking . . . is to be yourself. If you know your honest true self then it's the safest place you can inhabit. The only thing you really need to bring onto the podium and at the lectern is yourself — not rehearsed lines nor pages of notes. Remember the tale of the aforementioned Ms. Pirro. If she was open and practiced in improv – confident in her true self - then there would have never been the paralyzing fear that shut her vocal cords off for that long 45 seconds.

Improv is all about relationships. Human connection is the foundation. It strips every thing down to its simplest and most honest connection. If you are not connecting with your audience in quick, concise statements and thoughts then you will lose them. They are looking for and yearning for a connection with you. The same connections that you are. Again, they are in your corner. Please simply be honest with them.

We covered cold readings previously but a Staged Reading is another type of presentation all together. This can be an open mic type event or a directed reading of published work. Both allow time to familiarize yourself with the material and prepare the manner in which the work is to be presented. So there should be a level of comfort within the framework that can lend itself to a fearless performance. After all you have the written word in front of you and you simply have to read it. Right? Wrong! If anything this is where risk is not only encouraged but demanded. The danger with having a script in hand is that the performer can become complacent and the performance bland. Without costume and set the audience must really engage its active imagination to fill in the blanks. In order for them to do so you must be 110% invested in your own suspension of disbelief. In other words to convey wetness you must not only see the ocean from the deck of that ship but feel the coldness of the water as the spray of the surf hits you. If you know it to be true, then your audience will believe it with you. So don't be afraid to go big and make bold choices. Holding back because you fear that you will be seen as going over the top will only stifle your creativity and artistry. That kind of performance becomes nondescript, vague, dull...safe Have I said this before? You will be safe if you stay honest in the moment. Speak audaciously!

And now for something completely different

The job interview. An audition is basically a job interview. Granted this particular process of sitting face to face with human resources has a different set of rules and expectations than two minutes in front of an auditor. But you still need to put your best self forward if you want to be seriously considered for a position. In my mind the biggest difference is that at the job interview you can't walk in knowing beforehand exactly what you are going to say, as you have little to no control over what they are going to ask. So we all do our best to anticipate what may be asked and how to respond. We rehearse the expected questions with a pat answer. Walking in you know that they just have to ask *"What would you say is your greatest weakness?"* at some point. So you prepare the great comeback of: *"I get nervous when speaking in front of large groups."* Great answer. Honest but something that you can easily overcome with a little work and if you make sure you study the right 'self-help' book (insert a sly wink here).

But then they toss this curveball at you: *"What flavor would you be if you were ice cream?"* Egads! Are they serious? Are they trying to embarrass you? Well, to a certain extent, Yes! They aren't interested in a right or wrong answer (don't make me say it . . . we are too close to the end of this thing) but they do want to gauge your reaction to the unexpected. Or to see how easy it might be to fluster you. All of a sudden it is live theater and you have to improv. So, don't be afraid of taking a risk and being bold. *"Neopolitan, I like to think I celebrate diversity whenever given the chance."*

Or how about *"Name 5 Different Ways You Use A Pencil At Work."* Simply stay centered and calm. Approach it seriously even though it could be considered a fairly ridiculous question. *"1) Write, 2) Erase, 3) Tap it on the desk to release stress, 4) As a pointer when directing your attention and . . . uh . . . um . . . let me think for a second . . . OH, 5) Test the ceiling panels for their ability to hold onto a pointed object tossed straight up."* So #5 is a bit of a bold choice tossed into the batch for fun. An attempt at humor has the added benefit of letting them know you have a sense of one in potentially tense situations. Again, they aren't looking for the 'right' answer from this type of question. Because there isn't one! They expect you may have to think on your feet SO DO SO. Take your time. Start with the obvious and then let your improv skills take over.

"Why is a manhole cover round?" "So it will fit into the round hole in the street." What a simple honest answer.

My point here is you won't find anyway for you to prepare for these inane logic questions except to stay centered and relaxed. Be yourself. And perhaps most importantly, go in with the mindset that you are interviewing THEM. A job interview is . . . or should be . . . just as much a test for the company you are considering joining as it is a way for them to gauge if you might be the best candidate to come on board. And just like the offering of any role, you have the choice to turn it down if it doesn't feel right.

Most interviews end with *"Do you have any questions for us?* And a lot of people will defer and say something along the lines of, *"No you pretty much covered everything"* or *"I can't think of anything else."* But here is EXACTLY where your backstory and preparation come into play. As well as your confidence, focus and the trust in your honest self. It is the time for your pre-prepared text (or monologue if you will) and needs to be spoken in this present moment. Ask them, *"If we end up coming to an agreement that I am a great fit for you and you are a great fit for me, then I know I will want to succeede. What can you suggest to me that I accomplish in the next few months that would ensure a great rating at my first performance review? What is it that you look for that lets you know that you made the right decision in hiring me?"*

This type of question may be met with stunned silence. But just as you may have had a few thoughtful moments during the interview trying to figure out the best answer, this question will be one that they might have to give thought to before answering. Hopefully they will give you something honest about their expectations. If not, then you might have to consider that they failed their part in this test and you would be happier somewhere else.

First of all it tells them that you may be considering taking your valuable talent(s) elsewhere so their answer is just as important as any questions they may have put to you. But moreover it demonstrates a willingness on your part to be not only adaptable and flexible, but a desire on your part to make a difference in the world (Their world!). That you are sincere in your aspiration to find success within the script of the company. It tells them you are all about 99% commitment and 1% personal agenda (which you have left at the door). So was it your answers that mattered and landed the job? Or was it the question you posed to them that set you apart from all the other applicants who asked *"Do I get sick days?"* or *"How soon before I get a paid vacation?"*

Chapter Ten - Take a bow but duck that rotten tomato and mind the hook

Buckle up buttercup, it's about to get rough.

"Most people were heartless about turtles because a turtle's heart will beat for hours after it has been cut up and butchered" Ernest Hemingway

Full disclosure? The prior nine chapters are fraught with inconstancy and incongruency - accidentally on purpose with as much malice of forethought as I could muster. As best I could I remained positive, expressing helpful advice in an encouraging and supportive way. Often stated and purposefully overstated, there is no wrong or right when it comes to presenting your honest self on stage.

Now . . . in these final paragraphs . . . it's time to come clean. To tell the cold hard truth, and to let you in on the biggest baddest secret.

Ready?

The great unwashed, those sitting in both the cheap seats and the coveted boxes, brought not only tomatoes . . . but bucket loads of rotten, squishy, stinky cabbages. They ARE going to judge you. No matter how hard you work or how much invested you are in the script, the cast, the production and the success of the show. Even if they like the show they are going to go out for a drink afterwards and bitch about how much the tickets cost for such a lame evening of dreck. It's human nature and often it has more to do with their own failures than anyone or anything that they may have witnessed that evening. If they have a pen and notepad you can be certain that they will eviscerate you and your compatriots in the press. Blood red ink sells newspapers.

So you are going to suffer the slings and arrows of outrageous fortune(s). Know it. Accept it. Live it. Everybody's got an opinion and if they have a mean, nasty bone in there, they are going to dig it out, hollow it, poke holes in it and play it like a flute.

How to deal? The unfortunate truth it is you could have skipped all nine chapters and started here with Chapter Ten, and then closed the book. To put it in today's vernacular . . . ZFG . . . Zero. Fucks. Given. You have to have a hard shell if you are going to take that proverbial hook around the neck and survive the yank. But what about being in touch with honest emotions? Yeah yeah yeah, sensitivity is a tool you need to be able to pull out of the third drawer on the left hand side of your red rolling tool box in order to turn the screw that brings them to the point of standing on their feet clapping. But when it comes to being terrified of what ANYONE thinks of your work on stage gird your loins and break out the armor cause here come da judge. And as I've harped - no one - including yourself - has the right to judge you. Well yes they do. But it is your choice to let that affect your work in any sort of detrimental fashion. There is a difference between constructive criticism and some drunken patron sinking their dentures into your left buttock biting your ego in its ass. Remember the "mirror?" Let it go only that far and no farther. Constructive criticism should be coming from your director who is only trying to push you beyond your own limitations and finding the wherefore-all to risk. As you know by now, I wholeheartedly believe if you are unable to risk then get off the stage. You have no business being an actor and you should be terrified to step beyond the wings.

Remember I said Buckle up? I meant it.

But here are the niceties. Acting is easy. In the words of Noel Coward, "Speak clearly, don't bump into the furniture and if you must have motivation, think of your pay packet on Friday." And yes, I know that often in Community and Fringe theater your pay packet might be somewhat thinner than the envelope it comes in. And so, to quote Spencer Tracy "Learn you lines and don't trip over the furniture." Furthermore I should mention that Alfred Lunt explained blithely when asked the secret of being a fine actor, "I speak in a loud, clear voice—and keep from bumping into the furniture." In other words the best way to overcome stage fright (there's another broken promise) is to simply do the work that is required of you. Get off book and make notes regarding the blocking that is given you so you don't run over another actor. I directed a production of Tennessee William's "Night of the Iguana" at a community theater in eastern Oregon. Casting the show was a little difficult as I didn't have a huge talent pool from which to draw . . . and the range of experience in that talent wasn't all that wide. I ended up casting a fellow in the lead who looked great for the role and was 110 % committed to landing the part. But soon after the cast list was posted and quickly after the first table read, he started to express that he felt the line load was burdensome and his time on stage was overwhelming. I assured him that we would break everything down into bit sized chunks and he would have tons of support from the cast of 14. But this guy was so terrified of the role that he landed he couldn't do anything more than figure out his cues, lines and movement. All that was a terrifying chasm in front of him. So asking him to consider where his character's madness lie? It's enough to say that he emotional terrain he was willing to travel was at best level and most times downhill. But then the combined creativity of the production crew figured out an inspired way to present his slips into madness in a manner that didn't depend on the actor doing the background work . . . or honestly connecting with his inner demons . . . or finding triumph through adversity. A perfect example of everyone having everyone's back. Whenever the character's night terrors drove T. Larry Shannon to the end of his rope we had a musician placed behind the upstage curtain playing an eerily haunting instrument called a water phone. The sound of his madness tracked our intrepid actor's blocking across the stage. This trick actually freed the actor up and what could have easily be a disastrous production ended up being one of the most innovative endeavors that I (or perhaps he) had the pleasure of being a part of. Schism presented. Opportunity seized. Rather than judge the actor to be an incompetent failure, I found the resources to give him some relief from his self judgment. And the irony was that as soon as the pressure of "acting" was taken off his shoulders, and he was given audible cues as to when the character's terrors were overtaking him he was able to gain footing and skip across the thin rope bridge placed there for himself by himself. He was able to skip venturing up and down those valleys he was so terrified of during rehearsal. In retrospect, he got it. That actor trusted me and took on a willingness to risk it all. In the end he found just how easy it was to walk, talk, not bump into the furniture and chew up the scenery all at the same time, fearlessly.

I will reiterate something plainly stated earlier. Make

and define 'art' for yourself, not others. I am forced to create because I have to. It is intrinsically a part of who I am. That should be not only the driving force behind getting out on stage but also why judgment shouldn't be of any import to you. Whenever you call the art that you create "art" and your self an "Artist", then it simply is. The muse that speaks through you deems it art. And again, anyone who seeks to pass judgment is more than likely too frightened to do it themselves. Too risky. Why do they feel compelled to sit above what you have done . . . out of jealousy? An inability to do "it" themselves? More than likely, there lies a huge difference between criticism and heartfelt advice. This is why I hammered out the word 'trust' on my keyboard here time and time and time again. Trust yourself and your process. Trust those artists who support you and the work. Trust those who come to witness you creating art right in front of their eyes.

Another incongruence - Acting is work. Yes I know I just said it is easy. You just need to speak clearly and steer clear of the set dressing. But it doesn't need to be "hard." It can be "hard work" but "hard" does not have to mean difficult. I choose the word hard purposely because it is work that is done 24/7/52. Becoming and being an artist requires you to be in every moment. Dreams can be art. Or at least inspire it. A day in the park with your dog? . . . Art. If you can get to this spiritual place then 'art' and 'artist' require no definition. It just is. Why you do it is unimportant. It can be attributed to a need to connect with other humans, a narcissistic need for the applause, a way of explaining the world and politics, a desire to control something larger than yourself or a capitulation to that same great unknown. Whatever reason you may think you have for doing the work, the given is that there is a compulsion to do it that must be undertaken. If you didn't then you would walk around with a brokenness and a nagging feeling that you are less. You fall into judgment yet again. And that is reason enough. A reason why you need to wipe self judging out of your modus operandi. ESPECIALLY about the act of creation. If you are creating art in the present moment, which is the right way to do it, then there is no room for fear of doing it wrong. Any other way is a mistake.

And PLEASE don't limit yourself to the stage. The late great Red Skelton comes to mind, who was not only a comedic genius but also a painter. A camera in the hands of Dennis Hopper captured light in a voice of its own. Sam Shepard? Cowboy, and writer, playwright, director, actor. Finding expression outside the theater expands the how and the why you express yourself on stage. Remember way back when in the section on character building when I suggested that you seek inspiration from museums and music and novels? Become the inspiration. Let your inspiration come from your inner reveal. Paint, sing, play an instrument, write. Find that secondary muse that speaks to you and flows through you. Finding that sister muse will fulfill you not only in the interim between roles but team up on stage as well. It will help alleviate worry if you continually find the present moment that the act of creation is enmeshed in.

And while we are sort of on the subject . . . "Method" is bullshit. But if you find yourself cast as a cop if you don't ask your local police if you can do a ride along then you are short changing yourself. If you are cast as Cliff in "Woolgatherer", it would be nice if you actually knew what it felt like to be a long haul trucker, what the food at an interstate stop tasted like and the tricks you might use to outwit the scale stations along the way. What a pack-a-day

Marlboro man goes through to get from point A to point K in record time by driving all night high on bennies. Everything and anything that gets you comfortable in the skin of your character is fair game. Learn your lines and don't bump into the furniture unless you happen to be inhabiting the skin suit of Richard the Third, who must deal with a withered arm, hunched back and club foot. Then, by all means find a method that lets you figure out what he senses as he makes his way, as best he can, through his world. He might just bump into the throne as he makes his way to it and up on it. But that is one big bold specific choice now isn' it.

Finally, how presumptuous of me to tell you how to best go about getting over yourself. How impudent of me. I mean the audacity of this guy to tell you that the paralyzing fear that grips you can be overcome. And so maybe yes, it just is something that you have to come to terms with, and battle, and push through every time the curtain rises on your work. But hopefully I have at least given you some sort of road map complete with on and off ramps, highlighting heavy traffic and shortcuts around the jams. As I said starting out, acting is hard work that is so easy anyone should be able to do it.

Just do it.

About the Author: William has been involved in theater for over four decades working as Director, Producer, Playwright, Actor, Stage Manager, Designer and Dramaturge. Over those years he has served the Managing Director or Artistic Director of several fringe theater companies, in Oregon and Washington, as well as serving on the Steering Teams of several ongoing Theater Festivals and Arts Organizations. As an actor he has worked in everything from Musical Theater to Shakespeare to Original Work. He has been a guest lecturer at several Colleges in both Oregon and Washington. He is married to a wonderful playwright, director, artist and producer in her own right. Living in the Pacific Northwest with their amazing Shar-Pei who teaches them to answer this question daily, "How does this benefit the dog?"

Special Thanks go out to: my father who revealed to me that finding your muse and letting it possess you should never be fought against. To my Senior High Latin teacher who told me I never would be able to knowing that was all I needed to hear in order to prove her wrong. To Chris who taught me to bow to no man and call him King but to graciously accept a Queen's favor and return it unbloody. To Lisa who showed me that trembling in my boots was a reality that could be changed. To Suzanne who let me walk all over the alphabet, tap dancing from A to Z without worrying about M, S and W. To Heidi whose constructive criticism and unwavering support has literally saved my life on more than that one occasion. To ATUTI and 1448 who both examined my valise and found it to be too heavy, upending it and thereby making it easier to stop carting it around. To Scott, who forced me to put the jumble jigsaw together in a way that might make some semblance of an actual picture. And finally to Sadie, who demands I leave my personal agenda on the couch watching television without us while we explore worlds beyond the front door.

Made in the USA
Columbia, SC
23 November 2023

26968736R00065